Jumpstarters for Abbreviations

Short Daily Warm-ups for the Classroom

By
LINDA ARMSTRONG

ISBN 978-1-58037-570-2

Printing No. CD-404148

Visit us at www.carsondellosa.com

Mark Twain Media, Inc., Publishers
Distributed by Carson-Dellosa Publishing LLC

Table of Contents

Introduction to the Teacher

To succeed in today's competitive environment, students must improve their verbal skills. Quality classroom instruction remains the cornerstone of any instructional program, but experienced teachers know that learning requires reinforcement. This book offers teachers and parents short warm-up activities to help young readers and writers become proficient at recognizing and utilizing abbreviations. When used at the beginning of a language arts, mathematics, science, spelling, geography, or health and safety time-slot, these mini-tasks help students master this important communication skill.

The pages are grouped into units by topic. Types of abbreviations covered in this Jumpstarters collection include personal titles, geographical terms, addresses, measurements, technical terms, informal classified advertisement abbreviations, library terms, editing terms, and other common abbreviations used by writers. Each page features five mini-activities—one for each school day of the week.

Two main types of shortened words are presented in this book. They are abbreviations and acronyms. **Abbreviations** are shortened forms of words (Sept.). **Acronyms** are formed from the initials of several words in a title. (NATO) Technically, an acronym is read as a word. If an abbreviation is read as single letters (CEO), it is called an **initialization**.

> Before distributing the exercises, explain that abbreviations are short-cuts. In most cases, it is better to write out the word.

Encourage students to discover abbreviations used in text, on signs, on maps, on tables, and on the Internet. Invite them to notice that some words have different abbreviations for different uses. Many abbreviations have several different meanings. These shortened forms depend on context for clues to their meanings. To confuse things further, abbreviation rules are changing. Different publishers have different styles. For example, some style guides omit periods in abbreviations of academic degrees, and others do not.

This book devotes extra space to abbreviations that students will write often, such as personal titles and measurements. The rules for Mr., Mrs., and ft. are not disputed. Extra exercises help students spell and punctuate these common forms in appropriate contexts. Pages featuring more specialized abbreviations and acronyms focus on comprehension, rather than spelling and punctuation. Clues are offered in each exercise, but the use of dictionaries, texts, reference books, or the Internet is encouraged.

There are many ways to use this book.

- Reproduce the pages, cut along the lines, and use each section as a ten-minute warm-up or part of a homework assignment.
- Distribute copies of uncut pages so students can keep their completed exercises in a three-ring binder for reference.
- For use at a learning center, reproduce each page, cut the exercises apart, and mount each on a card with the corresponding answer key section on the back. Laminate for durability.
- Make transparencies or PowerPoint™ slides for group lessons
- Share the exercises in any order that fits your ongoing program.

Abbreviations Warm-ups: Part I: People and Places
Personal Titles

Name/Date ______________________

Personal Titles 1

Match the abbreviation to the full spelling.

____	1. Mr.	a.	Superintendent
____	2. Mrs.	b.	Doctor
____	3. Dr.	c.	Reverend
____	4. Supt.	d.	Mistress
____	5. Rev.	e.	Mister

Name/Date ______________________

Personal Titles 2

Circle the correct abbreviation.

1. Esquire — Eqr. Esq. Es.
2. Junior — Jr. Ju. Jn.
3. Senior — Se. Sn. Sr.
4. Doctor of Medicine — D.M. M.D. D.O.M.
5. Doctor of Dental Surgery — D.D.S. D.O.D. Dods.

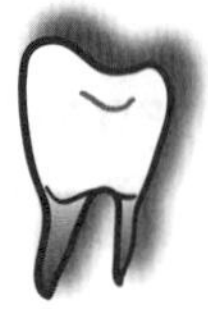

Name/Date ______________________

Personal Titles 3

Write the abbreviation. Note: Abbreviations are used only with both the first and last name.

1. Captain __________ William Peterson
2. General __________ Howard Wilson
3. Sergeant __________ Thomas Walker
4. Colonel __________ Jose Sandoval

Col. Capt. Gen. Sgt. Lt.

Name/Date ______________________

Personal Titles 4

On your own paper, write a sentence using each abbreviation or title.

1. Mr.
2. Mrs.
3. Dr.
4. Ms.
5. Miss (Hint: Do not use a period. This one is not an abbreviation.)

Name/Date ______________________

Personal Titles 5

Underline the usual meaning for each abbreviation.

1.	Ph.D.	Phone Doctor	Director of Phoenix	Doctor of Philosophy
2.	R.N.	Registered Nurse	Real Newsperson	Respected Nanny
3.	M.A.	Mean Angler	Master of Arts	Atlas Maker
4.	B.S.	Bachelor of Science	Bringer of Snacks	Best Singer
5.	B.A.	Best Artist	Best Archer	Bachelor of Arts

Note: These abbreviations are also correct without the periods.

Abbreviations Warm-ups: Part I: People and Places
Times, Places, and Directions

Name/Date ______________________________

Times, Places, and Directions 1

Write the abbreviations on the compass points.

______

West ______  ______

South ______

Choices: S Nth. N Wst. E W Est.

Name/Date ______________________________

Times, Places, and Directions 2

Write the meaning.

1. NP ______________________________
2. NM ______________________________
3. Natl. ______________________________
4. NF ______________________________
5. NWR ______________________________

Choices: National Monument, National, National Wildlife Refuge, National Park, National Forest

Name/Date ______________________________

Times, Places, and Directions 3

These are on a map. Circle the word in each list that best descibes the abbreviation.

1. Ft. Ross is a FAMILYTOWERFORTFREIGHTTRAIN
2. Pt. Reyes is a PRTPOINTTPAANGERNAMEPARTY
3. Raging R. is a RAKECITYVILLAGERIVERLAKERIOT
4. Sierra Nevada Mts. are MANAGEMNTMOUNTAINSMETERS
5. In St. Louis, St. stands for STREETSAINTSTARSSTANDARDS

Note: It is usually best to spell these words out.

Name/Date ______________________________

Times, Places, and Directions 4

Write each abbreviation for the time zone.

1. Pacific Daylight Time ____________
2. Mountain Standard Time ____________
3. Central Standard Time ____________
4. Eastern Daylight Time ____________
5. Pacific Standard Time ____________

Choices: MDT, CDT, EDT, PST, MST, CST, EST, PDT, GMT

Name/Date ______________________________

Times, Places, and Directions 5

Name the compass directions.

1. NE ____________________
2. NW ____________________
3. SE ____________________
4. SW ____________________
5. On another paper, draw a compass rose with eight points. Label the directions with abbreviations.

Abbreviations Warm-ups: Part I: People and Places
Continents and Countries

Name/Date ______________________________

Continents and Countries 1

Unscramble each abbreviated continent.

1. AF ______________________ FRAIAC
2. EU ______________________ UEEORP
3. SA ______________________ TUOHS MRAIAEC
4. AS ______________________ AASI
5. AN ______________________ RCAATTAICN
6. NA ______________________ RTNOH CAMIERA
7. AU ______________________ LTSRAIUAA

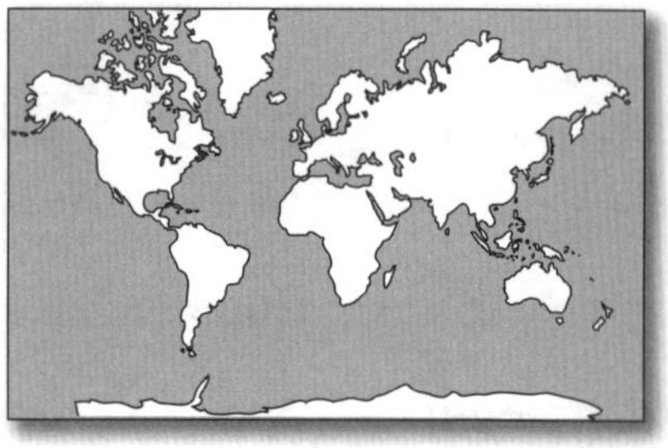

Name/Date ______________________________

Continents and Countries 2

Circle the correct abbreviation for each country.

1.	France	Fr.	Ger.	Isr.
2.	Netherlands	It.	Neth.	Swed.
3.	Algeria	Alb.	Alg.	Arg.
4.	Belgium	Aus.	Austral.	Belg.
5.	Brazil	Bol.	Braz.	Bulg.

Name/Date ______________________________

Continents and Countries 3

Fill in the missing letters of these abbreviated nations.

1. U.S. U __ __ t __ d S __ __ __ e __
2. U.K. U __ __ __ e __ Ki __ __ d __ __
3. Afgh. A __ __ __ a __ __ s __ __ n
4. Eth. Et __ __ o __ __ a
5. Hond. H __ __ __ u __ __ s

Name/Date ______________________________

Continents and Countries 4

Match the country to the correct abbreviation.

_____ 1. Jpn. a. Sweden
_____ 2. Lith. b. Norway
_____ 3. Swed. c. Portugal
_____ 4. Norw. d. Lithuania
_____ 5. Port. e. Japan

Name/Date ______________________________

Continents and Countries 5

Write the name of the country.

1. Can. ______________________
2. Col. ______________________
3. Dom. Rep. ______________________
4. Switz. ______________________
5. Thai. ______________________

Choices: Colombia, Switzerland, Canada, Thailand, Dominican Republic

Abbreviations Warm-ups: Part I: People and Places
Regions and States

Name/Date ______

Regions and States 1

The United States can be divided into four regions. Fill in the missing letters.

1. S S __ __ T __
2. NE N __ __ T __ E __ __ T
3. MW M __ __ W __ __ T
4. W W __ __ __
5. Write the abbreviation for your region. ______

Name/Date ______

Regions and States 2

Write the U.S. Postal Service's two-letter abbreviation for each state below.

1. Delaware ______
2. Arizona ______
3. Florida ______
4. Colorado ______
5. Georgia ______

Choices: AZ AR CA CO DA DE FL FO GA GE

Name/Date ______

Regions and States 3

Circle the state that matches each abbreviation below.

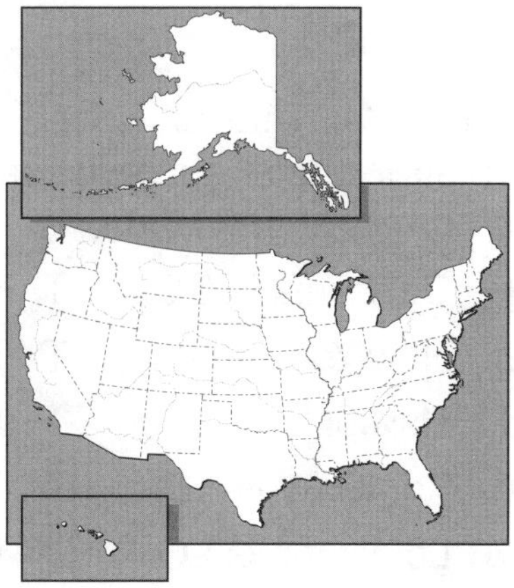

1.	HI	New Jersey	Kansas	Hawaii
2.	ID	Iowa	Idaho	Illinois
3.	IA	Iowa	Illinois	Kentucky
4.	KS	Kentucky	Kansas	Nevada
5.	LA	Virginia	Louisiana	Washington

Name/Date ______

Regions and States 4

Circle the abbreviated state.

1. ND NEWMEXICONORTHDAKOTA
2. NV NEWHAMPSHIRENEVADA
3. NH NEBRASKANEWHAMPSHIRE
4. NJ NEWJERSEYNEWMEXICO
5. NM NEBRASKANEWMEXICO

Name/Date ______

Regions and States 5

Circle the correct abbreviation for each state.

1.	Pennsylvania	RI	PA	PN
2.	Tennessee	TX	UT	TN
3.	Vermont	VT	VA	WA
4.	West Virginia	WI	WY	WV
5.	Oregon	DC	OG	OR

Abbreviations Warm-ups: Part I: People and Places
States

Name/Date ______________________________

States 1

Unscramble the bold word.

1. When should you always use two-letter abbreviations for states?
   WHEN YOU WRITE AN **DRADSES** ON AN ENVELOPE ______________
2. When should you always spell out the names of states?
   WHEN YOU USE A STATE NAME IN A **TNCESENE** ______________
3. Invent an address. Write the city and the state abbreviation. ______________
4. Use the name of your state in a sentence. ______________
   ____

Name/Date ______________________________

States 2

Circle T for True or F for False concerning two-letter postal abbreviations. If false, write the correct abbreviation.

1. California is CO. T F ________
2. New York is NY. T F ________
3. Hawaii is HA. T F ________
4. Kentucky is KE. T F ________
5. Louisiana is LO. T F ________

Name/Date ______________________________

States 3

Some charts use older state abbreviations. Match the old and new abbreviations.

_____ 1. Mass. a. AR
_____ 2. Miss. b. MT
_____ 3. Mont. c. MA
_____ 4. Tenn. d. TN
_____ 5. Ark. e. MS

Name/Date ______________________________

States 4

Circle the two-letter state abbreviations contained in the list below.

MIOUNESORTNMSINPNVVLAOMELMD
IMAAWACSCLWIGMNPDCUAZUNDOH
SOKKIASKSPKYOPAARICABCOIMOPP
ENHJNJJRIYVTSVABALMTCWYCTIDS
ILTRHISDPDEMFLDGAONYNCDAKTX
UTWVNM

Name/Date ______________________________

States 5

Unscramble the abbreviated states.

1. AR RKNAASAS ______________
2. TN NNSSTEEEE ______________
3. MS IIIISSSSMPP ______________
4. ME MINEA ______________
5. WY INYGOMW ______________

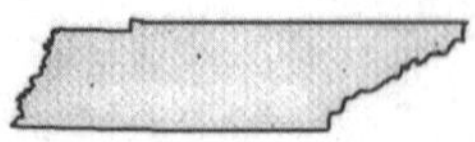

Abbreviations Warm-ups: Part I: People and Places
Highways and Streets

Name/Date ______________________

Highways and Streets 1

Write the correct abbreviation.

1. ___ ___ ___. Avenue
2. ___ ___. Street
3. ___ ___. Road
4. ___ ___ ___ ___. Boulevard
5. ___ ___. Drive

Choices: Blvd. St. Ave. Dr. Rd.

Name/Date ______________________

Highways and Streets 2

Fill in the missing letters.

1. Ct. C ___ ___ rt
2. Cl. ___ ir ___ l ___
3. Expy. E ___ p ___ ___ s ___ w ___ y
4. Ln. ___ ___ n ___
5. Pkwy. Pa ___ ___ w ___ ___

Name/Date ______________________

Highways and Streets 3

Circle the matching address for each abbreviation.

1.	Pl.	Place	Point	Pines
2.	Rt.	Rim	Route	Rise
3.	Sq.	Square	Street	Springs
4.	Terr.	Trail	Times	Terrace
5.	Aly.	Avenue	Annex	Alley

Name/Date ______________________

Highways and Streets 4

Unscramble each abbreviated address.

1. Frk. rfko ______________
2. Byp. yspabs ______________
3. Cp. apmc ______________
4. Cyn. nynoca ______________
5. Cv. oevc ______________

Name/Date ______________________

Highways and Streets 5

Underline the matching abbreviation for each location.

1.	Annex	Apt.	Ave.	Anx.
2.	Apartment	Anx.	Apt.	Ave.
3.	Basement	Bsmt.	Bldg.	Byp.
4.	Beach	Bldg.	Brg.	Bch.
5.	Building	Brg.	Bldg.	Bsmt.

6. Write the name of your school's street. ______________________

Abbreviations Warm-ups: Part I: People and Places Mixed Practice

Name/Date ______________________

People and Places Practice 1

Circle the matching abbreviation.

1. Europe UE EU Eup.
2. Department DE D.T. Dept.
3. Colorado C.O. CA CO
4. Spring Spg. SP S.P.
5. Avenue AV A.V.E. Ave.

Name/Date ______________________

People and Places Practice 2

Fill in the missing letters.

1. Mr. M ___ st ___ ___
2. FL Fl ___ r ___ ___ a
3. Hts. H ___ igh ___ s
4. Dr. D ___ ___ t ___ r
5. Mts. M ___ ___ n ___ ai ___ s

Name/Date ______________________

People and Places Practice 3

Unscramble the abbreviated words and write them on the lines.

1. St. teretS ______________________
2. Gdns. rsdGaen ______________________
3. Ph.D. ctoorD fo osohilypPh ____________ ______ ____________
4. HI aiwaHi ______________________
5. Capt. ntpiCaa ______________________

Name/Date ______________________

People and Places Practice 4

Write the word or words for each abbreviation.

1. Plns. ______________________
2. Sgt. ______________________
3. NV ______________________
4. Hwy. ______________________
5. D.D.S. ______________________

Choices: Doctor of Dental Surgery, Plains, Highway, Sergeant, Nevada

Name/Date ______________________

People and Places Practice 5

Match the correct abbreviation to the term.

_____	1. Doctor of Medicine	a.	D.D.S.
_____	2. Doctor of Philosophy	b.	M.S.
_____	3. Doctor of Dental Surgery	c.	M.D.
_____	4. Master of Arts	d.	Ph.D.
_____	5. Master of Science	e.	M.A.

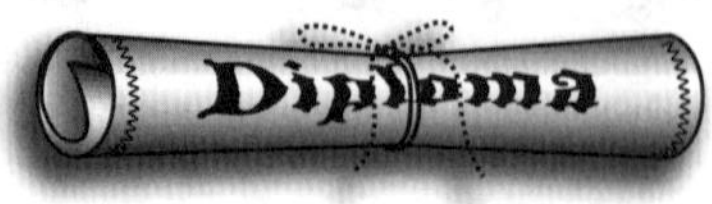

Abbreviations Warm-ups: Part I: People and Places Mixed Practice

Name/Date ____________________

People and Places Practice 6

Fill in the missing letters.

1. EST E __ __ te __ n St __ __ d __ __ d T __ __ e
2. ND N __ r __ h D __ k __ t __
3. MDT M __ __ nt __ in D__ __ lig __ t T __ __ e
4. NW No __ t __ we __ __
5. NJ N __ __ Je __ __ ey

Name/Date ____________________

People and Places Practice 7

Circle the post office abbreviations for these states.

Missouri, Washington, Utah, Pennsylvania, Maine, New Hampshire

UT St. Mrs. Dr. PA D.D.S.
Mr. WA M.A. NH MDT ME
B.A. Sr. Hwy. MO EST Jr.

Name/Date ____________________

People and Places Practice 8

Write the abbreviation for the underlined word or words.

1. Senior George Smith, ________
2. Mistress ________ Helene Foster
3. Doctor of Philosophy Harold Thomas, ________
4. Junior Martin James, ________
5. Boulevard Hayward ________

Name/Date ____________________

People and Places Practice 9

Fix all errors. Write the correct version on the line.

1. mr Edward Collins ________
2. phd Stewart Martin ________
3. jr George Williams ________
4. mrs Tanya Anderson ________
5. dr Elena Gonzalez ________

Name/Date ____________________

People and Places Practice 10

Circle the best choice for each.

1. In Los Angeles, CA 90042, CA stands for — a personal title / a street suffix / a state name
2. In Dr. Kelly Richards, Dr. stands for — a personal title / a street suffix / a state name
3. In 223 West Blvd., Blvd. stands for — a personal title / a street suffix / a state name
4. In Mr. Carson Martin, Mr. stands for — a personal title / a street suffix / a state name
5. In Grand Junction, CO 81501, CO stands for — a personal title / a street suffix / a state name

Abbreviations Warm-ups: Part I: People and Places Mixed Practice

Name/Date ______________________

People and Places Practice 11

On another paper, use each title in a sentence.

1. Mr. 2. Dr.
3. Mrs. 4. Ms.
5. Miss
6. Which one never uses a period?

____

Name/Date ______________________

People and Places Practice 12

Correct this, and write it as an address for an envelope:

mr Jason West
223 Hill Avue
Los Angeles, Calfrnia 90040

____

____

____

Name/Date ______________________

People and Places Practice 13

Circle the best match for each title.

1. D.D.S.	a teacher	an artist	a dentist
2. M.D.	a dentist	a physician	an electrician
3. Jr.	a son	a daughter	a wife
4. Mrs.	a son	a husband	a wife
5. Mr.	a man	a woman	a girl

Name/Date ______________________

People and Places Practice 14

Match each term to the correct abbreviation.

_____	1. Mr.	a. Master of Science
_____	2. AZ	b. Boulevard
_____	3. Blvd.	c. Department
_____	4. M.S.	d. Arizona
_____	5. Dept.	e. Mister

Name/Date ______________________

People and Places Practice 15

Invent an address. Use a title, a name, a street address, a city, a state, and a zip code.

____

____

____

____

Abbreviations Warm-ups: Part II: Measurement
Hours, Minutes, Days

Name/Date ______________________________

Hours, Minutes, Days 1

Circle the best match for the meaning of the abbreviation. These abbreviations may also appear as small caps (A.M. and P.M.) or all caps with no periods (AM and PM).

1.	2–4 p.m.	morning	morning to afternoon	afternoon
2.	11 a.m.–2 p.m.	morning	morning to afternoon	afternoon
3.	10 a.m.–4 p.m.	morning	morning to afternoon	afternoon
4.	8–10 a.m.	morning	morning to afternoon	afternoon
5.	3–5 p.m.	morning	morning to afternoon	afternoon

Name/Date ______________________________

Hours, Minutes, Days 2

Write the day for each abbreviation.

1. Mon. ________________
2. Thurs. ________________
3. Sat. ________________
4. Weds. ________________
5. Tues. ________________
6. Sun. ________________
7. Fri. ________________

Name/Date ______________________________

Hours, Minutes, Days 3

Underline the correct abbreviation.

1.	Eastern Daylight Time	EST	EDT
2.	Central Standard Time	CST	CDT
3.	Mountain Daylight Time	MST	MDT
4.	Pacific Daylight Time	PST	PDT

5. Write your current time zone.

____

Name/Date ______________________________

Hours, Minutes, Days 4

Unscramble the matching word for each abbreviation.

1.	hr.	oruh	________________
2.	min.	nuemti	________________
3.	sec.	doecns	________________
4.	M	nodyaM	________________
5.	F	raFyid	________________

Name/Date ______________________________

Hours, Minutes, Days 5

Use each abbreviation to write a time.
Example: 2:20 p.m.

1. a.m. ________________
2. p.m. ________________
3. PM ________________
4. AM ________________
5. Is 6:32 a.m. in the morning or at night?

____

Abbreviations Warm-ups: Part II: Measurement Months

Name/Date ______________________________

Months 1

Match each month or word to the correct abbreviation.

_____	1. mos.	a. March
_____	2. Jan.	b. April
_____	3. Feb.	c. months
_____	4. Mar.	d. January
_____	5. Apr.	e. February

Name/Date ______________________________

Months 2

Fill in the missing letters for each month.

1. Oct. O __ __ o __ __ r
2. Dec. D __ __ e __ __ e __
3. Aug. A __ __ __ s __
4. Nov. N __ v __ __ b __ __
5. Sept. S __ __ __ e __ __ __ r

Name/Date ______________________________

Months 3

Find and circle the month in each row.

1. Apr. APRICOTAPRILAPPLYAPPLE
2. Jan. JANISJANUARYJAPANJNUR
3. Aug. GIAUGUSTAUNDAYEDPND
4. Oct. OCTAGONOCTOBEROVERD
5. Feb. FEDFEBRUARYFETHRUARYO

Name/Date ______________________________

Months 4

Use abbreviations to fill in the table.

Spring	Summer	Fall	Winter
Mar.	Jun.	Sept.	Dec.

Name/Date ______________________________

Months 5

MARCH						
	1	2	3	4	5	6
7	8	9	10	11	12	13
14	15	16	17	18	19	20
21	22	23	24	25	26	27
28	29	30	31			

Write True or False for each statement below.

1. The abbreviation Mar. is often used on calendars. ______________
2. The abbreviation Sept. is often used in sentences. ______________
3. The abbreviation Dec. is often used on charts. ______________
4. The abbreviation Jan. is often used on appointment cards. ______________
5. The abbreviation Oct., like Mr., is always used. ______________

Abbreviations Warm-ups: Part II: Measurement
Years, Centuries, Millennia

Name/Date ___

Years, Centuries, Millennia 1 Unscramble the word that goes with each abbreviation. These abbreviations may also appear in small caps: AD, BCE, etc.

1. AD ANON ODINMI ___
2. BC FOEBRE RITCSH ___
3. BCE FOREBE OMNCMO RAE ___
4. CE NOMCMO AER ___
5. C RYNTCEU ___

Name/Date ___

Years, Centuries, Millennia 2
Fill in the missing letters.

1. M is the abbreviation for M ___ l ___ en ___ ___ m.
2. The year 79 BC is part of the f ___ ___ st c ___ nt ___ ry BC.
3. The year 213 BCE was 213 years B ___ f ___ ___ e the C ___ ___ ___ on E ___ ___.
4. The year ___ ___ 79 is in the first century of the Common Era.

Name/Date ___

Years, Centuries, Millennia 3
Study each time span. Cross out the date that is not included.

1. Oct. 12–14 Oct. 13 Dec. 4 Oct. 14
2. Nov. 28–Dec. 10 Nov. 26 Dec. 1 Nov. 30
3. Apr. 6–15 Apr. 11 Apr. 17 Apr. 14
4. Jan. 2–Mar. 22 Feb. 3 Mar. 12 Mar. 29

Name/Date ___

Years, Centuries, Millennia 4
Fill in missing numbers, punctuation marks, or letters.

1. The class of '10 graduated in 2 ___ ___ ___.
2. The year 1985 was part of the 1 ___ ___ 0s.
3. The year 1882 was part of the 18 ___ ___s.
4. The flood of '08 happened in 2 ___ ___ ___.
5. The oil spill was one of 2010 ___ ___ most important events.

Name/Date ___

Years, Centuries, Millennia 5
Which came first? Underline the earliest date in each pair.

1. CE 200 100 BCE
2. Nov. 12, 2003 Jan. 22, 2004
3. 345 BC AD 341
4. 1880s 1980s
5. Write a date that came before Apr. 2, 2000. ___

Abbreviations Warm-ups: Part II: Measurement
Metric Measures

Name/Date ______________________________

Metric Measures 1

Circle the matching metric measurement that goes with each abbreviation.

1. g — geology — German — gram
2. kg — kilogram — karate — Kansas
3. mcg — machine — microgram — memory card
4. mg — milligram — mark — Monday
5. MT — mountain — metric ton — Montana
6. Are abbreviations for metric measurements followed by a period? Y N

Name/Date ______________________________

Metric Measures 2

Match the abbreviation to the correct measurement.

_____	1. bit	a. GB
_____	2. byte	b. TB
_____	3. kilobyte	c. b
_____	4. gigabyte	d. KB
_____	5. terabyte	e. B

Name/Date ______________________________

Metric Measures 3

Write the matching metric liquid measurements.

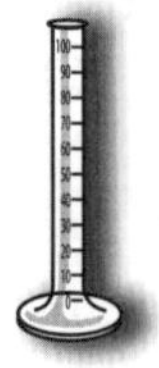

1. L ____________________
2. cL ____________________
3. dL ____________________
4. kL ____________________
5. mL ____________________

Choices: kiloliter, centiliter, liter, milliliter, deciliter (These may also be abbreviated with a lowercase l: cl, ml, etc.)

Name/Date ______________________________

Metric Measures 4

Unscramble the measurement that goes with each abbreviation.

1. mm ERMELITMIL ____________________
2. cm EENTIRCMET ____________________
3. km OMEKTEILR ____________________
4. m ERTEM ____________________
5. dm TEEECIRDM ____________________

Name/Date ______________________________

Metric Measures 5

Find and circle the measurement that goes with the abbreviation in each row.

1. W ttwwirllwonstwattwonrkwoaitwishi
2. kW kilowattkeeptpspellkentwashworkle
3. kWh kow-tow-kilowatt-hour-yue-stre-am
4. K KperKiKngKelvinKinderKgarten
5. C CafCfeineCallmCelsiusCuruulus

Abbreviations Warm-ups: Part II: Measurement
Standard Measures

Name/Date ____________________

Standard Measures 1

Fill in the missing letters.

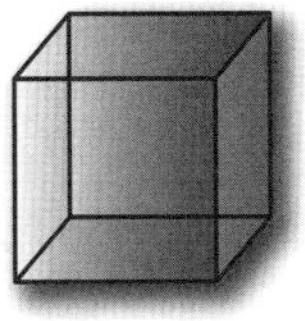

1. sq. s _ _ _ r _
2. cu. _ u _ _ c
3. doz. d _ _ e _
4. rpm r _ _ ol _ t _ _ n _ p _ _ m _ _ u _ _
5. mph _ i _ _ s p _ _ h _ _ _

Name/Date ____________________

Standard Measures 2

Match each word to the correct abbreviation.

____	1. in.	a. length
____	2. ft.	b. mile
____	3. yd.	c. foot
____	4. mi.	d. yard
____	5. l.	e. inch

6. Abbreviations for standard measures are followed by a period. Y N

Name/Date ____________________

Standard Measures 3

Find a chart of standard measures; write True or False for each statement.

1. The abbreviation *oz.* stands for the word *ounce.* ____________
2. The abbreviation *lb.* stands for *liberty.* ____________
3. The abbreviation *T.* stands for *ton.* ____________
4. The abbreviation *pt.* stands for *pint.* ____________
5. The abbreviation *qt.* stands for *quiet.* ____________

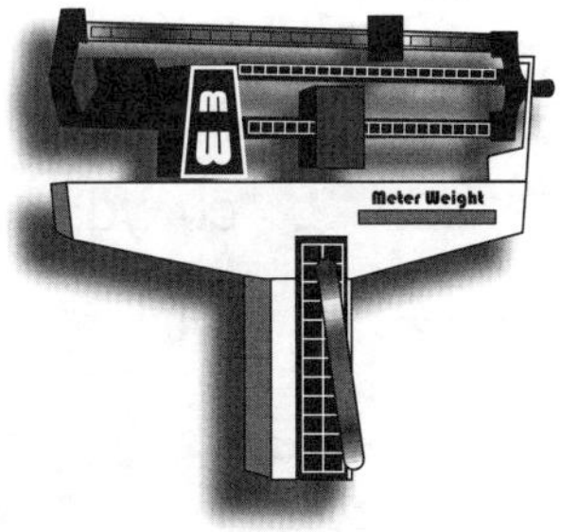

Name/Date ____________________

Standard Measures 4

Find a cookbook; fill in the missing letters.

1. tsp. t _ _ _ p _ _ n
2. tbsp. _ a _ _ _ s _ _ o _
3. c. _ u _
4. gal. _ _ l _ _ n
5. F F _ h _ _ n _ ei _

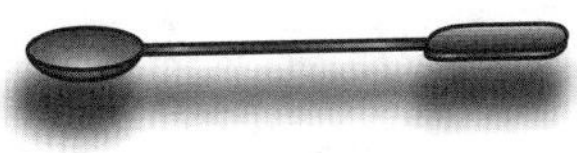

Name/Date ____________________

Standard Measures 5

Fill in the blank with the correct measurement.

1. n.m. ____________
2. kt. ____________
3. mph ____________
4. qt. ____________
5. ft. ____________

Choices: feet, miles per hour, nautical miles, quart, knot

Abbreviations Warm-ups: Part II: Measurement
Standard Measures of Length

Name/Date ____________________

Standard Measures of Length 1

Circle the correct abbreviation. (Hint: ′ stands for feet, and ″ stands for inches.)

1.	36″	YD	yd.	yrd.
2.	12″	ft.	FT	Ft
3.	5,280′	MI	Mi	mi.
4.	1″	IN	in.	Ich.

Name/Date ____________________

Standard Measures of Length 2

Fill in the missing letters.

1. sq. mi. s _ u _ r _ m _ l _
2. sq. in _ q _ _ _ e _ _ ch
3. sq. yd. _ _ u _ r _ _ _ _ d
4. sq. ft. _ _ _ a r _ f _ _ t
5. These abbreviations are found in lists and on charts. T F

Name/Date ____________________

Standard Measures of Length 3

Match the measurement to the correct abbreviation.

_____ 1. cu. mi. a. cubic yard
_____ 2. cu. ft. b. cubic foot
_____ 3. cu. yd. c. cubic mile
_____ 4. cu. in. d. cubic inch

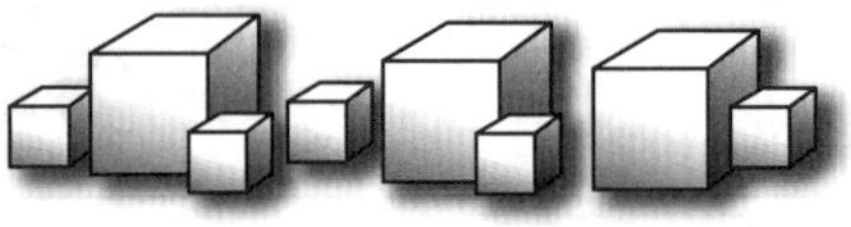

Name/Date ____________________

Standard Measures of Length 4

Fill in the missing measurement abbreviations.

1. 12″ = 1 ________ 2. 3′ = 1 ________
3. a block of ice 1′ on each edge contains 1 ________ ________
4. a sheet of paper 8″ on each side contains 64 ________ ________
5. a floor 12′ on each side contains 144 ________ ________

Name/Date ____________________

Standard Measures of Length 5

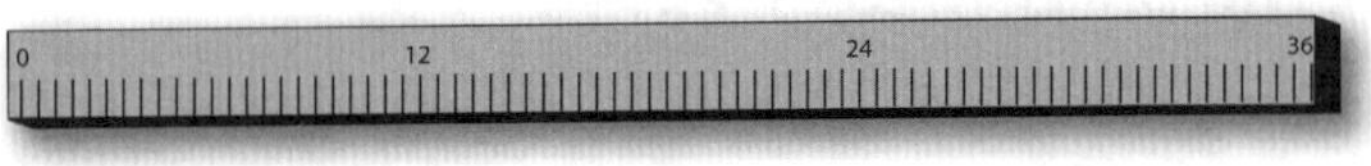

Write True or False for each statement.

1. The abbreviation *sq. mi.* would be used to describe the size of a wall. ____________
2. The abbreviation *cu. ft.* would be used to describe the air space in a building. ____________
3. The abbreviation *sq. yd.* would be used to describe a sheet of notebook paper. ____________
4. The words *square miles* would be used in a newspaper story about a forest fire. ____________
5. The abbreviation *cu. in.* would be used to label items on a chart. ____________

Abbreviations Warm-ups: Part II: Measurement
Standard Measures of Volume

Name/Date ____________________

____

Standard Measures of Volume 1

Invent a recipe. List the ingredients. Use abbreviations for the following measures:

teaspoon, tablespoon,
cup, pint, quart

[Hint: The ingredients can be silly, but the abbreviations must be correct.]

____

____

____

____

____

____

____

____

____

____

____

____

Name/Date ____________________

Standard Measures of Volume 2

Write the abbreviation for each measurement.

1. quart ________
2. pint ________
3. tablespoon ________
4. gallon ________
5. cup ________

Choices: c., tbsp., pt., qt., gal.

Name/Date ____________________

Standard Measures of Volume 3

Fill in the missing measurement abbreviations.

1. 8 fl. oz. = 1 ________
2. 2 c. = 1 ________
3. 2 pt. = 1 ________
4. 4 qt. = 1 ________
5. 3 tsp. = 1 ________

Choices: qt. pt. tbsp. c. gal.

Name/Date ____________________

Standard Measures of Volume 4

Circle the match for the abbreviation in each row.

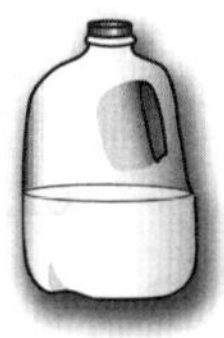

1. c. QUARTGALLONPINTINCHCUP
2. pt. QUARTPINTFOOTGALLONCUP
3. qt. QUARTSPOONGALLONCUPPINT
4. gal. QUARTYARDGALLONCUPPINT
5. Of four containers, circle the largest: pt. qt. c. gal.

Name/Date ____________________

Standard Measures of Volume 5

What's probably inside? Circle the best choice.

1.	$\frac{1}{2}$ fl. oz.	perfume	milk
2.	1 c.	gasoline	detergent
3.	1 qt.	gasoline	milk
4.	15 gal.	perfume	gasoline
5.	1 pt.	perfume	cream

Abbreviations Warm-ups: Part II: Measurement
Standard Measures Mixed Practice

Name/Date ______________________________

Standard Measures Mixed Practice 1

Fill in the word for the abbreviation in each sentence.

1. 2 T. The truck weighed two ____________.
2. 78°F The water was 78° ____________.
3. 6 oz. Just six ____________ of milk remained.
4. 2 lb. She bought two ____________ of flour.
5. 3 tsp. He added three ____________ of sugar.

Name/Date ______________________________

Standard Measures Mixed Practice 2

Circle the correct measure for each abbreviation.

1.	oz.	ovens	ounce	oranges
2.	lb.	pound	latitude	liberty
3.	T.	Tennessee	ton	teaspoon
4.	doz.	pound	ounces	dozen

Name/Date ______________________________

Standard Measures Mixed Practice 3

Fill in the missing letters.

1. oz. o __ __ c __
2. lb. __ ou __ __
3. T. __ __ n
4. tsp. te __ __ __ o __ n
5. tbsp. t __ __ le __ __ __ __ n

Name/Date ______________________________

Standard Measures Mixed Practice 4

Circle the correct hidden measure in each row.

1. in. OUNCEFOOTINCHCHINLB
2. oz. YAPOUNCEENPOUNDTON
3. lb. NDPOPOUNDOUNCWINYD
4. yd. YDRFOOTLBPOUNYARDTON
5. T. TIMESTONRTEASPONDOZLB

Name/Date ______________________________

____

Standard Measures Mixed Practice 5

List the measurements of an imaginary monster. Use abbreviations.

1. Length from nose to tip of tail
   ____
2. Height
   ____
3. Total weight
   ____
4. Length of front teeth
   ____
5. Length of tail
   ____

Draw your monster on your own paper. Label the drawing.

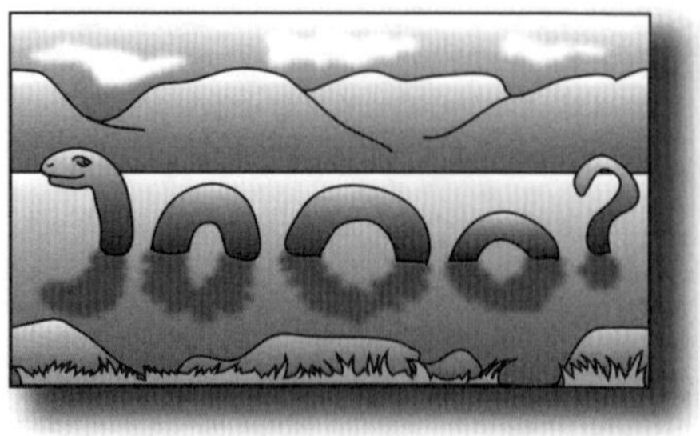

Abbreviations Warm-ups: Part II: Measurement Metric and Standard Mixed Practice

Name/Date ____________________

Metric & Standard Mixed Practice 1

Match the measurement to the correct abbreviation.

_____	1. in.	a. meters
_____	2. cm	b. millimeters
_____	3. mm	c. inches
_____	4. ft.	d. centimeters
_____	5. m	e. feet

Name/Date ____________________

Metric & Standard Mixed Practice 2

What would each measure? Circle the most likely item.

1. mi.	a trip	a rug
2. km	a table	a marathon
3. yd.	a football field	a paper clip
4. m	a mouse's tail	a hallway
5. ft.	a tree	eyeglasses

Name/Date ____________________

Metric & Standard Mixed Practice 3

Fill in the missing letters.

1. L   l __ t __ __
2. qt.   q __ __ __ t
3. pt.   p __ __ __
4. mL   __ i __ __ __ li __ __ r
5. kL   __ __ __ o __ __ __ er

Name/Date ____________________

Metric & Standard Mixed Practice 4

Write the abbreviation for each measure.

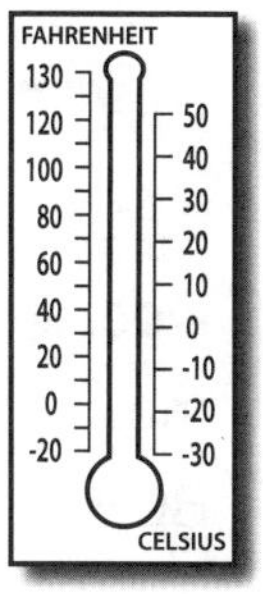

1. Fahrenheit __________
2. Celsius __________
3. ounce __________
4. pound __________
5. gram __________

Name/Date ____________________

Metric & Standard Mixed Practice 5

Imagine a garden. Fill in your information. Use abbreviations for the following:

Celsius, centimeters, liters, millimeters, meters

1. Length of the garden ____________________
2. Amount of water in the fish pond ____________________
3. Temperature of the pond ____________________
4. Length of the largest fish ____________________
5. Length of the smallest flower seed ____________________

Abbreviations Warm-ups: Part II: Measurement
Time Mixed Practice

Name/Date ____________________

Time Mixed Practice 1

Circle the best abbreviation.

1.	Monday	Mdy.	Mon.
2.	hour	hr.	HR
3.	Eastern Standard Time	EST	ET
4.	Anno Domini	AD	DA
5.	Before Common Era	BComE	BCE

Name/Date ____________________

Time Mixed Practice 2

Match the term to the correct abbreviation.

_____	1. BC	a. Tuesday
_____	2. CDT	b. November
_____	3. Tues.	c. ante meridiem
_____	4. Nov.	d. Before Christ
_____	5. a.m.	e. Central Daylight Time

Name/Date ____________________

Time Mixed Practice 3

Unscramble. (Hint: Some are more than one word.)

1. PDT htTiicDmPaligcifaye ____________________
2. p.m. edpieitmmosr ____________________
3. Dec. beecmrDe ____________________
4. mo. onhtm ____________________
5. BCE onrrBeeCmamEfoo ____________________

Name/Date ____________________

Time Mixed Practice 4

Circle the abbreviation meaning the opposite of the first item in each line.

1.	**AD**	BC	AM	PM
2.	**p.m.**	AD	CDT	a.m.
3.	**BCE**	CE	MST	p.m.
4.	**a.m.**	PST	p.m.	BCE
5.	**BC**	BCE	p.m.	AD

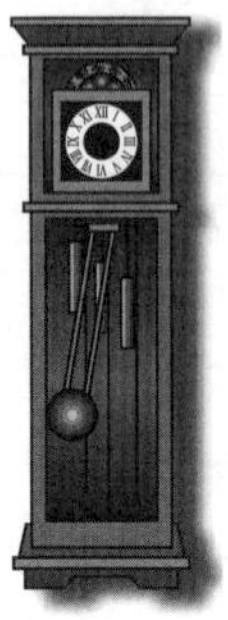

Name/Date ____________________

Time Mixed Practice 5

Use abbreviations to write

1. a date ____________________
2. a time in the morning ____________________
3. a time in the afternoon ____________________
4. any year before the Common Era ____________________
5. a time during the summer on the Pacific coast ____________________

Abbreviations Warm-ups: Part II: Measurement Mixed Practice

Name/Date ______________________________

Measurement Mixed Practice 1

Circle the best choice.

1.	PDT	Pacific Daylight Time	Perfect Daylight Time	pound
2.	lb.	liter	pound	long ton
3.	tsp.	Pacific Standard Time	Celsius	teaspoon
4.	MST	measurements	Mountain Standard Time	tablespoon
5.	a.m.	ante meridiem	anno Domini	after May

Name/Date ______________________________

Measurement Mixed Practice 2

Match the measure to the correct abbreviation.

_____	1. CST	a.	Celsius
_____	2. Jan.	b.	kilogram
_____	3. kg	c.	liter
_____	4. L	d.	Central Standard Time
_____	5. C	e.	January

Name/Date ______________________________

Measurement Mixed Practice 3

Fill in the abbreviation for each measurement.

1. quart ____________
2. kilometer ____________
3. yard ____________
4. gallon ____________
5. pint ____________

Name/Date ______________________________

Measurement Mixed Practice 4

Unscramble the measurements.

1. mm LIMEERMILT ____________
2. tbsp. OAPOENBLTS ____________
3. F ENRAHIHEFT ____________
4. c. UPC ____________
5. Feb. EBFARUYR ____________

Name/Date ______________________________

Measurement Mixed Practice 5

Write abbreviations for months of the year.

1. ____________ 2. ____________
3. ____________ 4. ____________
5. ____________ 6. ____________
7. ____________ 8. ____________
9. ____________ 10. ____________
11. ____________ 12. ____________

Abbreviations Warm-ups: Part II: Measurement Mixed Practice

Name/Date ____________________

Measurement Mixed Practice 6

Find and circle the word or words that match the abbreviation in each row.

1. Mar. MARGOMARCHMAGAZINE
2. BC KMLBEFORECHRISTBACK
3. ft. FEETINCHYARDFEELING
4. Tues. THURSDAYTIMETUESDAY
5. min. MRTMINUTEMINNOWMAY

Name/Date ____________________

Measurement Mixed Practice 7

Fill in the meaning of each abbreviation.

1. Oct. ____________________
2. kL ____________________
3. yr. ____________________
4. gal. ____________________
5. cu. ____________________

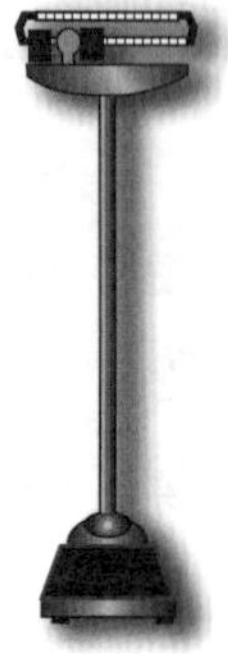

Name/Date ____________________

Measurement Mixed Practice 8

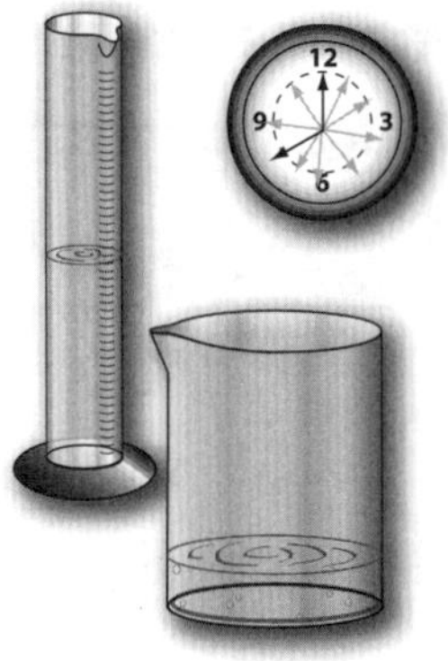

What came first? Underline the earliest date or time in each row.

1.	9:35 a.m.	2:15 p.m.	6:20 a.m.
2.	Mar. 21	Oct. 15	Feb. 16
3.	CE 241	215 BCE	CE 465
4.	Feb. 21, 2009	Feb. 10, 2010	Feb. 20, 2008
5.	9:20 p.m.	11:42 a.m.	10:15 a.m.

Name/Date ____________________

Measurement Mixed Practice 9

Unscramble the words that match the abbreviations.

1. Dec. CEMERBDE ____________________
2. Thurs. TURYSDAH ____________________
3. qt. ARQUT ____________________
4. min. NIEUTM ____________________
5. Feb. RURYAFEB ____________________

Name/Date ____________________

Measurement Mixed Practice 10

Write abbreviations for the days of the week.

1. ____________ 2. ____________
3. ____________ 4. ____________
5. ____________ 6. ____________
7. ____________

Abbreviations Warm-ups: Part II: Measurement Mixed Practice

Name/Date ______________________________

Measurement Mixed Practice 11

Circle the abbreviation that could label each.

1.	a length	gm	ft.	c.
2.	a weight	in.	lb.	gal.
3.	an amount of liquid	gal.	mm	yd.
4.	the size of a floor	oz.	sq. ft.	T.
5.	the air space in a room	cu. ft.	lb.	tsp.

Name/Date ______________________________

Measurement Mixed Practice 12

Fill in the missing letters.

1. km K __ L __ M __ __ __ R
2. gal. __ __ L __ __ N
3. yd. Y __ __ __
4. mm __ __ __ __ __ I __ __ T __ R
5. pt. __ __ __ T

Name/Date ______________________________

Measurement Mixed Practice 13

Match each abbreviation to the correct measurement.

_____ 1. meter a. qt.
_____ 2. square foot b. m
_____ 3. quart c. kg
_____ 4. mile d. sq. ft.
_____ 5. kilogram e. mi.

Name/Date ______________________________

Measurement Mixed Practice 14

Unscramble the equivalent measurements.

1. 1,000 m OMETKILER ______________
2. 4 qt. OGALNL ______________
3. 5,280 ft. ILEM ______________
4. 100 cm TERME ______________
5. 1,000 g LOKRAIGM ______________

Name/Date ______________________________

Measurement Mixed Practice 15

Use abbreviations to write:

1. a time in the afternoon ______________
2. an amount of liquid ______________
3. a date this year ______________
4. a year more than 2,050 years ago ______________
5. a time in the Rocky Mountains ______________

Abbreviations Warm-ups: Part III: Science and Technology—Health and Medicine

Name/Date ______________________

Health and Medicine 1

Match each term to the correct abbreviation.

_____	1. BMI	a.	computed tomography
_____	2. cal.	b.	cubic
_____	3. cc	c.	body mass index
_____	4. CT	d.	calorie
_____	5. cu	e.	cubic centimeter

Name/Date ______________________

Health and Medicine 2

Fill in the missing letters.

1. pH a m _ _ _ _ re of ac _ _ i _ y
2. ppm p _ _ _ s p _ r m _ _ l _ _ n
3. ppt p _ _ ts p _ _ t _ i _ _ _ on
4. pos p _ _ it _ _ e
5. neg _ _ g _ t _ _ e

Name/Date ______________________

Health and Medicine 3

Unscramble the meaning of each abbreviation.

1. dB IBCLEDE ______________
2. temp. MPATUEERTER ______________
3. M LAMRO ______________
4. BP LOBOD ESRPRSUE ______________
5. CT CUTEOMPD TOAPGRYHMO ______________

Name/Date ______________________

Health and Medicine 4

Fill in the meaning of each abbreviation.

1. EKG ______________
2. f. ______________
3. m. ______________
4. M.D. ______________
5. DNA ______________

Choices: female, Doctor of Medicine, male, deoxyribonucleic acid, electrocardiogram

Name/Date ______________________

Health and Medicine 5

Circle the term that matches the abbreviation in each row.

1. MRI MROMIRRNMAGNETICRESONANCEIMAGINGIERMST
2. wt. HEIGHTWEIGHTBOOKWAITINGWAYEIMNBRWLBN
3. F FARNEARMAGNETICHEATFAHRENHEITSIZESFARDLO
4. hosp. HOSTIHOSTESMHOLISHOORGPPHOPINSPELHOSPITAL
5. HMO ORHEALTHMAINTENANCEORGANIZATIONHELTHP

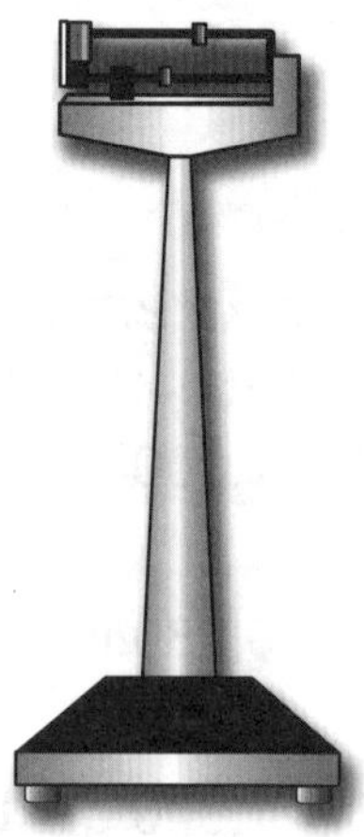

Abbreviations Warm-ups: Part III: Science and Technology—Weather

Name/Date ______________________________

Weather 1

Fill in the missing letters in the cloud types.

1. Cs c _ r _ o _ tr _ t _ s
2. Ci c _ r _ us
3. Cb cu _ _ lon _ _ b _ _
4. Ac a _ _ ocu _ _ l _ _
5. Cu c _ m _ l _ s

Choices: cumulonimbus, altocumulus, cirrostratus, cumulus, cirrus

Name/Date ______________________________

Weather 2

Match the term to the correct abbreviation.

_____	1. St	a. advisory
_____	2. F	b. stratus
_____	3. C	c. broken
_____	4. ADVY	d. Fahrenheit
_____	5. BKN	e. Celsius

Name/Date ______________________________

Weather 3

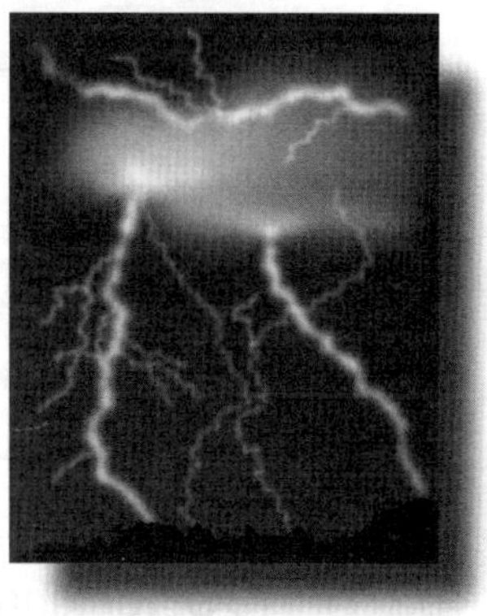

Circle the meaning of each abbreviation.

1. in.	inches	inside
2. ft.	Fahrenheit	feet
3. LTNG	lightning	limits
4. OBS	oblong system	observation
5. NWS	Nice Winter Snow	National Weather Service

Name/Date ______________________________

Weather 4

Fill in the meaning of each Weather Service abbreviation.

1. CLR ______________________
2. DRZL ______________________
3. FRZN ______________________
4. GSTS ______________________
5. HLSTO ______________________

Choices: gusts, frozen, clear, hailstones, drizzle

Name/Date ______________________________

Weather 5

Unscramble each NWS abbreviation.

1. FG OGF ______________
2. TS URDOTHNRMEST ______________________
3. SH OHRWESS ______________
4. DS USDT TSRMO ______________
5. RA INRA ______________

Abbreviations Warm-ups: Part III: Science and Technology—Elements

Name/Date ______________________

____

Elements 1

Fill in the elements that make up each compound.

1. H_2O (water)
   ______________________,
   ____
2. NaCl (table salt)
   ______________________,
   ____
3. CO_2 (carbon dioxide)
   ______________________,
   ____
4. Fe_2O_3 (rust)
   ______________________,
   ____
5. $NaHCO_3$ (baking soda)
   ______________________,
   ______________________,
   ______________________,
   ____

Hints: Na: sodium, H: hydrogen, O: oxygen, Cl: chlorine, Fe: iron, C: carbon

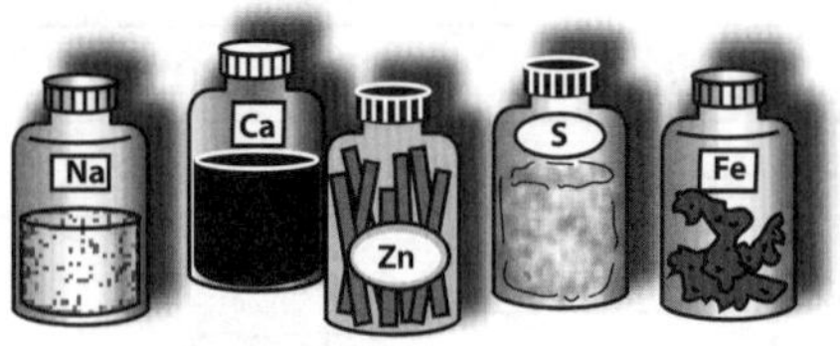

Name/Date ______________________

Elements 2

Circle the element that goes with each abbreviation.

1.	Al	barium	argon	aluminum
2.	Am	americium	calcium	arsenic
3.	Ar	argon	calcium	silver
4.	Ba	calcium	boron	barium
5.	Ca	hydrogen	calcium	carbon

Name/Date ______________________

Elements 3

Match the element to the correct abbreviation.

_____	1. Co	a. hydrogen
_____	2. C	b. helium
_____	3. He	c. cobalt
_____	4. H	d. oxygen
_____	5. O	e. carbon

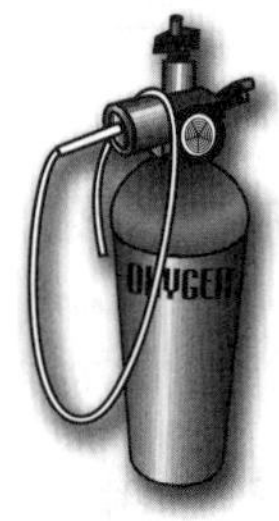

Name/Date ______________________

Elements 4

Fill in the blank letters for each element.

1.	I	i _ d _ _ e
2.	S	s _ _ fur
3.	Zn	z _ _ c
4.	B	b _ _ _ n
5.	Cu	c _ p _ _ r

Choices:
copper
iodine
zinc
boron
sulfur

Name/Date ______________________

Elements 5

Circle the hidden element that goes with each abbreviation.

1.	Au	angdelpragoldsdfomurelkgbuianklewfjlst
2.	Si	siliconsillyaougsilentstsimpleoimslopestro
3.	U	unusualunderunableuraniumugmusuala
4.	Ag	silverageagricultureangelgoldeaglearmy
5.	Cl	colorcleanclickchlorinechorusclicleaclips

Abbreviations Warm-ups: Part III: Science and Technology—Communications

Name/Date ____________________

Communications 1

Fill in the blank with the correct term.

1. dpi ____________________
2. FTP ____________________
3. GIF ____________________
4. GPS ____________________

Choices: dots per inch, file transfer protocol, global positioning system, graphic interchange format

Name/Date ____________________

Communications 2

Match the term to the correct abbreviation.

____ 1. UHF ____ 2. HTML

____ 3. HTTP ____ 4. FAQ ____ 5. IP

a. frequently asked questions
b. internet protocol
c. ultrahigh frequency
d. hypertext markup language
e. hypertext transfer protocol

Name/Date ____________________

Communications 3

Circle the correct abbreviation for each term.

1. international unit OW ST IU
2. optical character recognition OCR BCE ODR
3. operating system OM OS OG
4. personal computer CO PR PC
5. Uniform Resource Locator URL RES LOC

Name/Date ____________________

Communications 4

Fill in the missing letters.

1. DVD d _ _ it _ l v _ _ eo d _ _ c
2. cps c _ _ les p _ r se _ _ nd
3. VHF v _ _ y h _ _ _ fr _ _ _ e _ _ y
4. elec. el _ _ t _ _ c
5. RAM ra _ _ om a _ _ e _ _ m _ _ o _ _

Choices: very high frequency, electric, digital video disc, random access memory, cycles per second

Name/Date ____________________

Communications 5

Fill in the missing word that is the other half of each portmanteau word.

1. e-zine = electronic + ____________________
2. e-mail = electronic + ____________________
3. Internet = international + ____________________
4. freeware = free + ____________________
5. transistor = transfer + ____________________

Choices:
network
resistor
software
mail
magazine

Abbreviations Warm-ups: Part III: Science and Technology—Space Science

Name/Date ____________________

Space Science 1

Fill in the term that goes with each abbreviation.

1. lt-yr — light-__________
2. MVEMJSUNP — Mercury, Venus, Earth, Mars, __________, Saturn, Uranus, Neptune, Pluto
3. VLF — very low __________
4. VLA — very large __________
5. WD — __________ dwarf

Choices:
array
white
frequency
Jupiter
year

Name/Date ____________________

Space Science 2

Unscramble the constellations.

1. And — romAdenda __________
2. Aqr — usquriaA __________
3. Cnc — narceC __________
4. CMi — asniC Mrino __________
5. Cas — aseaCsioip __________

Name/Date ____________________

Space Science 3

Match the term to the correct abbreviation.

_____ 1. RF _____ 2. NS
_____ 3. deg _____ 4. JPL
_____ 5. IR

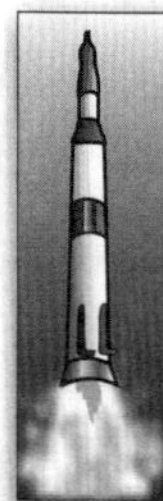

a. Jet Propulsion Laboratory
b. degree c. neutron star
d. infrared e. radio frequency

Name/Date ____________________

Space Science 4

Fill in the missing letters.

1. sat — s _ t _ _ li _ e
2. UT — _ ni _ _ rsal _ im _
3. CG — _ _ n _ _ r of g _ _ v _ _ y
4. g — gra _ i _ y
5. HF — h _ _ h fre _ u _ n _ y

Name/Date ____________________

Space Science 5

Fill in the blanks with the missing words.

1. BBT — __________ Bang Theory
2. NASA — National Aeronautics and __________ Administration
3. gxy — __________
4. KBO — Kuiper Belt __________
5. AU — Astronomical __________

Choices: galaxy, Units, Object, Space, Big

Abbreviations Warm-ups: Part III: Science and Technology—Mixed Practice

Name/Date ________________________

Science and Technology Practice 1

Match the term to the correct abbreviation.

_____ 1. ac _____ 2. ASCII

_____ 3. bps _____ 4. Btu

_____ 5. cps

a. British thermal unit b. bits per second
c. American Standard Code for Information Interchange
d. cycles per second e. alternating current

Name/Date ________________________

Science and Technology Practice 2

Fill in the scientific terms.

1. geol. ________________
2. no. ________________
3. ac ________________
4. atm ________________
5. bp ________________

Choices: alternating current, boiling point, number, atmosphere, geology

Name/Date ________________________

Science and Technology Practice 3

Supply the missing letters in these scientific terms.

1. cm ce _ t _ me _ _ r
2. cp c _ _ dl _ po _ er
3. CPU ce _ _ _ al p _ o _ _ s _ _ ng u _ _ t
4. mp m _ _ ti _ g po _ _ t
5. KE kin _ _ ic en _ _ gy

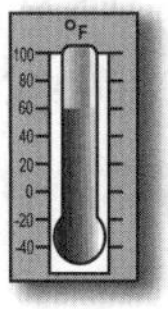

Name/Date ________________________

Science and Technology Practice 4

Unscramble the words that match each abbreviation.

1. Hz ehzrt ________________
2. rpm onvretiolus per minute ________________
3. m meret ________________
4. V ovtl ________________
5. std radadnst ________________

Name/Date ________________________

Science and Technology Practice 5

Fill in the missing words.

1. dpi ________________ per inch
2. MIDI Musical ________________ Digital Interface
3. ppm ________________ per million
4. dc ________________ current
5. IU International ________________

Choices:
instrument
parts
unit
dots
direct

Abbreviations Warm-ups: Part III: Science and Technology—Mixed Practice

Name/Date ______________________

Science and Technology Practice 6

Fill in the missing word.

1. RF ____________ frequency
2. NS neutron ____________
3. deg ____________
4. JPL ________ Propulsion Laboratory
5. IR ____________

Choices: Jet, degree, infrared, star, radio

Name/Date ______________________

Science and Technology Practice 7

Match the term to the correct abbreviation.

___	1.	BBT	a.	Kuiper Belt Object
___	2.	NASA	b.	galaxy
___	3.	gxy	c.	National Aeronautics and Space Administration
___	4.	KBO		
___	5.	AU	d.	Astronomical Units
			e.	Big Bang Theory

Name/Date ______________________

Science and Technology Practice 8

Circle the constellation that matches each abbreviation.

1.	And	Aquarius	Cancer	Andromeda
2.	Aqr	Canis Minor	Aquarius	Cassiopeia
3.	Cnc	Cancer	Canis Minor	Andromeda
4.	CMi	Cancer	Aquarius	Canis Minor
5.	Cas	Aquarius	Cancer	Cassiopeia

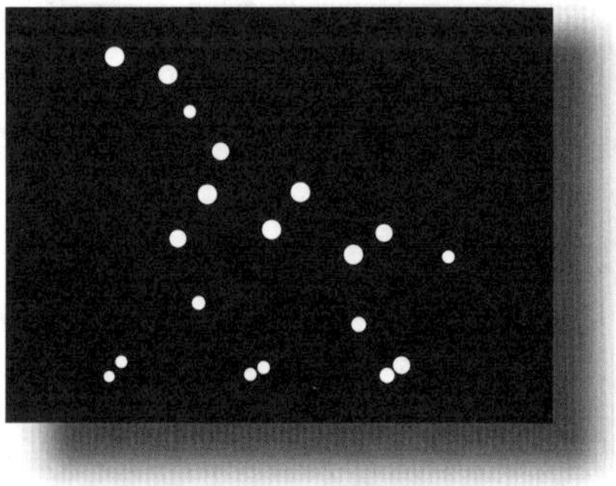

Name/Date ______________________

Science and Technology Practice 9

Write the terms that match these abbreviations.

1. UHF ____________
2. dpi ____________
3. IP ____________
4. FAQ ____________
5. GPS ____________

Name/Date ______________________

Science and Technology Practice 10

Circle the meaning.

1.	in.	inches	inside
2.	ft.	Fahrenheit	feet
3.	LTNG	lightning	limits
4.	OBS	orbital	observation
5.	NWS	New Weather Story	
		National Weather Service	

Abbreviations Warm-ups: Part IV: Common Acronyms and Initializations

Name/Date ____________________

Acronyms and Initializations 1

Fill in the missing words.

1. NASA ____________ Aeronautics and Space Administration
2. SCUBA self-contained ____________ breathing apparatus
3. LASER light amplification by stimulated emission of ____________
4. ROM read ____________ memory
5. SNAFU situation ____________ all fouled up

Choices: only, radiation, underwater, normal, National

Name/Date ____________________

Acronyms and Initializations 2

Fill in the missing letters.

1. RADAR rad __ __ d __ __ ec __ __ on and rang __ __ g
2. AWOL a __ sent with __ __ t l __ __ ve
3. RAM ra __ do __ a __ __ e __ s me __ __ r __
4. ATM a __ __ __ mat __ d te __ __ er ma __ __ i __ e

Name/Date ____________________

Acronyms and Initializations 3

Unscramble the bold print word.

1. COD cash on **veyderli** ____________
2. PIN **sorlnape** identification number ____________
3. CEO chief executive **feicofr** ____________
4. ZIP zone improvement **alpn** ____________

Name/Date ____________________

Acronyms and Initializations 4

Circle T for True or F for False.

T F 1. A BLT is a flying saucer.

T F 2. You will get TLC when you are sick.

T F 3. A UFO is a sandwich with tomatoes.

T F 4. Many people watch shows on TV.

T F 5. TBA means *to be announced.*

Name/Date ____________________

Acronyms and Initializations 5

Match each term to the correct initialization.

____ 1. R.S.V.P. ____ 2. S.A.S.E.

____ 3. RV ____ 4. PS

____ 5. AKA

a. recreational vehicle b. postscript

c. also known as d. répondez s'il vous plaît

e. self-addressed stamped envelope

Abbreviations Warm-ups: Part IV: Common Acronyms and Initializations

Name/Date ____________________

____

Acronyms and Initializations 6

Circle the missing word.

1. ASAP	as soon as ____
   pleasing parade possible
2. CEO	chief ____ officer
   executive editing earning
3. CPA	certified public ____
   accountant artist actor
4. FYI	for your ____
   insight improvement information
5. HQ	____quarters
   head happy healing

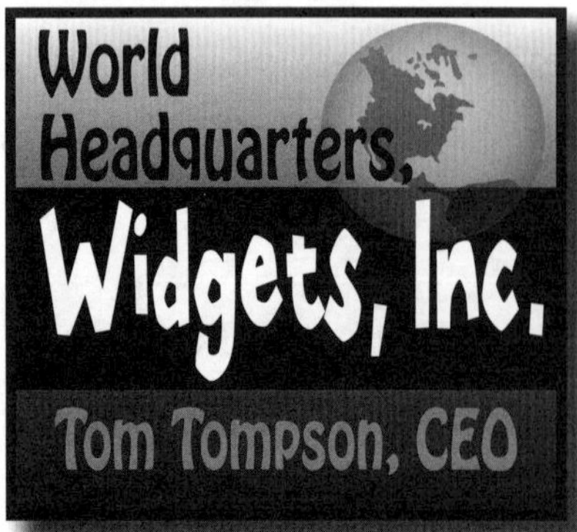

Name/Date ____________________

Acronyms and Initializations 7

Fill in the missing letters.

1. CPU	cen _ _ _ l pr _ _ ess _ _ g u _ _ _
2. PA	p _ _ lic ad _ _ e _ s
3. ZIP	zo _ e imp _ _ ve _ _ nt p _ _ n
4. TBA	to be a _ _ ou _ _ _ d
5. SUV	s _ _ _ t u _ _ li _ y v _ _ i _ _ e

Name/Date ____________________

Acronyms and Initializations 8

Fill in the blank.

1. SOS	save our ____________
2. TV	____________
3. VIP	very ____________ person
4. SRO	____________ room only
5. PDQ	pretty darn ____________

Choices:
television
quick
standing
ship
important

Name/Date ____________________

Acronyms and Initializations 9

Circle T for True or F for False.

T F 1. IOU means *I owe you.*
T F 2. FAQ means *fish and quail.*
T F 3. FYI means *for your imagination.*
T F 4. MIA means *missing in action.*
T F 5. MYOB means *make your own bread.*

Name/Date ____________________

Acronyms and Initializations 10

Unscramble the word in bold.

1. AKA	also **onwkn** as	____________
2. DJ	disc **eoyjck**	____________
3. NA	not **licleapabp**	____________
4. PS	post **rtipsc**	____________
5. TLC	tender **vginlo** care	____________

Abbreviations Warm-ups: Part V: Writing Words About Words

Name/Date ____________________

Words About Words 1

Match each word to the correct abbreviation.

_____	1. n.	a. adverb
_____	2. v.	b. preposition
_____	3. adj.	c. verb
_____	4. adv.	d. adjective
_____	5. prep.	e. noun

Dog (n): Canine

Name/Date ____________________

Words About Words 2

Write the word for each abbreviation.

1. suff. ____________
2. pron. ____________
3. usu. ____________
4. sp. ____________
5. pronunc. ____________

Choices: pronoun, spelling, usually, pronunciation, suffix

Name/Date ____________________

Words About Words 3

Circle the meaning of each abbreviation.

1. part.	partnership	preposition	participle
2. conj.	connection	conjunction	compound
3. obj.	object	observation	obvious
4. syll.	superlative	suffix	syllable
5. superl.	superior	superlative	syllable

Name/Date ____________________

Words About Words 4

Fill in the missing letters.

1. pr. pple. pr _ _ e _ t p _ _ tic _ _ le
2. sing. si _ _ ul _ r
3. pres. pr _ _ e _ _
4. pref. pr _ _ _ x
5. poss. po _ _ e _ _ i _ e

Name/Date ____________________

Words About Words 5

Unscramble.

1. pl. lurlap ____________
2. compar. maetivpacor ____________
3. pa.t. satp neste ____________
4. syn. oysynmn ____________
5. ant. oynatmn ____________

Abbreviations Warm-ups: Part V: Writing Other Dictionary Terms

Name/Date ____________________

Other Dictionary Terms 1

Circle the dictionary term for each abbreviation.

1.	dial.	dial	dialect	dictionary
2.	dict.	dictionary	dialect	during
3.	dim.	dim	diminutive	dialect
4.	esp.	except	spelling	especially
5.	exc.	except	extra	extended

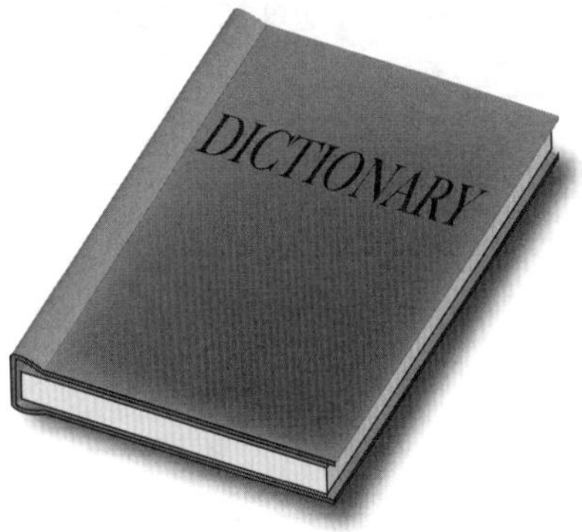

Name/Date ____________________

Other Dictionary Terms 2

Match each term to the correct abbreviation.

_____ 1. abbrev. a. compound

_____ 2. colloq. b. definition

_____ 3. cpd. c. demonstrative

_____ 4. def. d. colloquial

_____ 5. dem. e. abbreviation

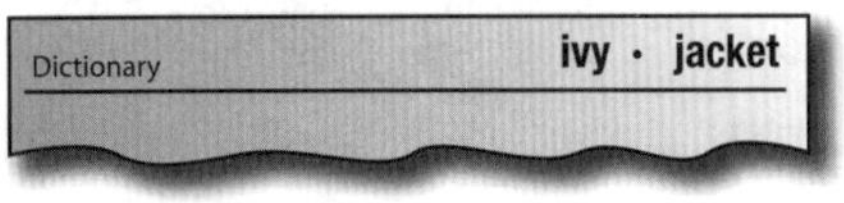

Name/Date ____________________

Other Dictionary Terms 3

Fill in the missing letters.

1. cpd. c _ _ po _ nd
2. dial. di _ le _ t
3. exc. e _ c _ _ t
4. freq. f _ _ qu _ _ tly
5. inf. inf _ _ it _ _ e

Name/Date ____________________

Other Dictionary Terms 4

Write the word for each abbreviation.

1. unkn. ____________
2. techn. ____________
3. std ____________
4. pop. ____________
5. phr. ____________

Choices: popularly, phrase, technical, unknown, standard

Name/Date ____________________

Other Dictionary Terms 5

Unscramble the abbreviated word.

1. inf. nivetinfii ____________
2. irreg. egarirulr ____________
3. misc. oclaumisneles ____________
4. occas. olcnaasiolcy ____________
5. abbrev. tibaonrevabi ____________

abbrev. (n) a shortened form of a written word

Abbreviations Warm-ups: Part V: Writing Latin Terms and Shortened English Words

Name/Date ____________________

Latin Terms/English Words 1

Match each meaning to its Latin abbreviation.

____ 1. i.e. (*id est*) ____ 2. etc. (*et cetera*)

____ 3. vs. (*versus*) ____ 4. ibid. (*ibidem*)

____ 5. e.g. (*exempli gratia*)

a. and so forth b. for example

c. in the same book or passage

d. that is e. against

Name/Date ____________________

Latin Terms/English Words 2

Circle the meaning of each Latin abbreviation.

1. et al. (*et alii*) and others about
2. id. (*idem*) the same about
3. R.I.P. (*requiescat in pace*)
   and others rest in peace
4. ad lib (*ad libitum*)
   improvise rest in peace
5. ca. (*circa*) improvise about

Name/Date ____________________

Latin Terms/English Words 3

Circle T for True or F for False.

T F 1. n.b. (*nota bene*) means *to pay close attention.*

T F 2. R. can mean *rex* (king) or *regina* (queen).

T F 3. prox. (*proxima*) means a tall building.

T F 4. PS (*postscriptum*) stands for the date on a letter.

T F 5. pro. tem. (*pro tempore*) means *for the time being.*

Name/Date ____________________

Latin Terms/English Words 4

Fill in the missing letters.

1. ex. ex __ __ p __ e
2. no. n __ __ b __ r
3. fig. fi __ __ r __
4. ed. ed __ t __ __ n
5. esp. es __ __ ci __ __ ly

Name/Date ____________________

Latin Terms/English Words 5

Write the meaning of each Latin abbreviation.

1. ad infin. *ad infinitum* ____________________
2. Q.E.D. *quod erat demonstrandum* ____________________
3. cf. *confer* ____________________
4. con. *contra* ____________________
5. non seq. *non sequitur* ____________________

Choices: against, compare, continuing forever, does not follow, so it is shown

Abbreviations Warm-ups: Part V: Writing Words About Publications

Name/Date ______________________

Words About Publications 1

Fill in the missing words.

1. TOC table of ________
2. TP ________ page
3. c. copy________
4. pp ________
5. gloss. ________

Choices: glossary, pages, title, contents, right

Name/Date ______________________

Words About Publications 2

Circle the hidden word that goes with each abbreviation.

1. p. anddpagextbleofcntrlakpan
2. chap. chapteroneperfecttrnslation
3. pref. quottionlkecinprefacetentsm
4. tr. translationpagestableoconp
5. anon. seriesqutitlepaganonymous

Name/Date ______________________

Words About Publications 3

Unscramble the word for each abbreviation.

1. rev. reedvis ________
2. Ser. iersSe ________
3. quot. untiotaqo ________
4. Publ. ubtioslicPan ________
5. Q. rrlatyeQu ________

Name/Date ______________________

Words About Publications 4

Fill in the missing letters of each word.

1. mag. m __ g __ zi __ e
2. illus. il __ __ __ tr __ __ i __ n
3. add. ad __ __ n __ a
4. intro. i __ tr __ __ u __ __ i __ n
5. bib. bi __ __ io __ __ a __ __ y

Name/Date ______________________

Words About Publications 5

Match each word to the correct abbreviation.

____	1. hist.	a. gazette
____	2. myst.	b. figure (chart or illustration)
____	3. gaz.	c. historical
____	4. fig.	d. biography
____	5. biog.	e. mystery

Abbreviations Warm-ups: Part VI: Career Track Business and Finance

Name/Date ______________________

Business and Finance 1

Circle T for True or F for False.

T F 1. COD usually means *cash on delivery.*

T F 2. Assn. means *action.*

T F 3. Org. means *organization.*

T F 4. Dept. means *deep water.*

T F 5. Bros. means *brothers.*

Name/Date ______________________

Business and Finance 2

Widgets, Inc. W

Fill in the missing letters.

1. Co. Co _ _ a _ y
2. Corp. Co _ _ or _ _ i _ n
3. Inc. I _ co _ _ o _ a _ _ d
4. LP Limited P _ _ _ ner _ _ ip
5. Ltd. Li _ _ t _ d

Name/Date ______________________

Business and Finance 3

Unscramble the word for each abbreviation.

1. Mfg. nufrinacmatug ______________________
2. RR adilraro ______________________
3. Ry ilyawra ______________________
4. mgr. mgnaera ______________________
5. mdse. haseemcndir ______________________

Name/Date ______________________

Business and Finance 4

Match each word to the correct abbreviation.

_____	1. div.	a. amount
_____	2. recd.	b. building
_____	3. amt.	c. received
_____	4. asst.	d. assistant
_____	5. bldg.	e. division

Sunny Decks, Inc. Invoice # 2056
June 1 - Recd. on account: $325.00

Name/Date ______________________

Business and Finance 5

Circle the business word that goes with each abbreviation.

1. acct.	accomplished	account	accumulate
2. ea.	each	early	easy
3. incl.	increase	inside	including
4. pd.	paid	pick	place
5. pkg.	part	paid	package

Abbreviations Warm-ups: Part VI: Career Track
Classified Ads

Name/Date ______________________________

Classified Ads 1

Fill in the job title for each abbreviation.

1. atty. ____________________
2. vet. ____________________
3. asst. ____________________
4. mgr. ____________________
5. prin. ____________________

Choices: principal, assistant, manager, veterinarian, attorney

Name/Date ______________________________

Classified Ads 2

Match each term to the correct abbreviation.

____	1. ref.	a. full time
____	2. f.t.	b. experience
____	3. p.t.	c. references
____	4. temp.	d. temporary
____	5. exper.	e. part-time position

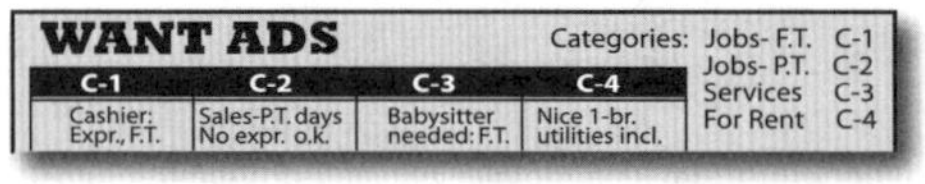

Name/Date ______________________________

Classified Ads 3

Unscramble the bold word.

1. CPA certified public **cnontauact** ____________________
2. LPN licensed **acapctirl** nurse ____________________
3. K **hontusad** ____________________
4. IT **iormanntiof** technology ____________________
5. ref. **efcererens** ____________________

Name/Date ______________________________

Classified Ads 4

Circle T for True or F for False.

T F 1. hrs. p.w. means *hours per week.*

T F 2. sal. means *solid.*

T F 3. reqd. means *required.*

T F 4. approx. means *exactly.*

T F 5. bkgd. means *building.*

Name/Date ______________________________

Classified Ads 5

Fill in the missing letters.

1. Sat/Sun Sa __ __ rd __ y and Su __ __ ay
2. M–F Mo __ __ ay through F __ __ __ ay
3. pd. vac. paid va __ __ ti __ __ s
4. appt. ap __ __ in __ __ e __ t
5. pers. dept. p __ __ s __ __ nel dep __ __ __ m __ __ t

Abbreviations Warm-ups: Part VI: Career Track Organizations, Companies, Agencies, and Acts

Name/Date ______________________

Organizations, Companies, Agencies, and Acts 1

Match each agency to the correct abbreviation.

_____ 1. SBA _____ 2. NOAA _____ 3. FDA
_____ 4. FAA _____ 5. ACF

a. Federal Aviation Administration b. Food and Drug Administration c. Small Business Administration
d. Administration for Children and Families
e. National Oceanic and Atmospheric Administration

Name/Date ______________________

Organizations, Companies, Agencies, and Acts 2

Circle the correct abbreviation.

1. American Broadcasting System ABC CAB CBA
2. Columbia Broadcasting System BSC SCB CBS
3. National Broadcasting Company BNC NBC CBN
4. Public Broadcasting System PBS BSP SBP
5. British Broadcasting Corporation CCB BBC BCB

Name/Date ______________________

Organizations, Companies, Agencies, and Acts 3

Unscramble the bold word.

1. UPS United Parcel **erevSic** __________
2. FedEx **dealrFe** Express __________
3. USPS United States **sltPoa** Service __________
4. ADA Americans with **aesilbtiiDis** Act __________
5. NPR National **cuPlib** Radio __________

Name/Date ______________________

Organizations, Companies, Agencies, and Acts 4

Fill in the missing letters.

1. EU E __ __ op __ __ n Union
2. NATO North Atlantic Treaty O __ __ ani __ a __ __ on
3. UN U __ __ __ ed N __ tions
4. OPEC Organization of P __ tro __ __ __ m-Exporting Countries

UN

Name/Date ______________________

____

Organizations, Companies, Agencies, and Acts 5

Fill in the missing word.

1. CIA Central __________ Agency
2. FBI Federal Bureau of __________
3. IRS __________ Revenue Service
4. EEOC Equal Employment Opportunity __________
5. OSHA __________ Safety and Health Administration

Choices: Internal, Commission, Occupational, Investigation, Intelligence

Abbreviations Warm-ups: Part VI: Career Track Education

Name/Date ____________________

Education 1

Unscramble the bold word.

1. IRA International **ienRadg** Association ____________
2. NSF National **ccieSen** Foundation ____________
3. NCTE National Council of Teachers of **hligsEn** ____________
4. NAEA National Art Education **ionAsocatis** ____________
5. NCSS National Council for the **claSoi** Studies ____________

Name/Date ____________________

Education 2

Fill in the missing word.

1. AP ____________ Placement
2. ELL English Language ____________
3. ESL English as a Second ____________
4. IEP Individualized ____________ Plan
5. NCLB No ____________ Left Behind

Choices: Language, Child, Advanced, Learner, Education

Name/Date ____________________

Education 3

Circle the abbreviation for each degree.

1. Bachelor of Arts B.F.A. B.A. B.E.E.
2. Bachelor of Electrical Engineering B.F.A. B.A. B.E.E.
3. Bachelor of Fine Arts B.F.A. B.A. B.E.E.
4. Bachelor of Nursing B.N. C.E. B.F.A.
5. Civil Engineer B.N. B.F.A. C.E.

Name/Date ____________________

Education 4

Match the term to the correct abbreviation.

_____ 1. AD _____ 2. ASL

_____ 3. GATE _____ 4. GED

_____ 5. GPA

a. General Education Diploma
b. Gifted and Talented Education
c. Athletic Director d. Grade Point Average
e. American Sign Language

Name/Date ____________________

Education 5

Circle T for True or F for False.

T F 1. A *K–12* school includes 11th grade.

T F 2. *NHS* stands for *National Honor Society.*

T F 3. The *NEA* includes people interested in education.

T F 4. In *PE,* students learn about poetry.

T F 5. The *USDOE* helps farmers grow better crops.

Abbreviations Warm-ups: Part VI: Career Track Sports

Name/Date ____________________

Sports 1

Fill in the missing letters.

1. NBA National B _ _ _ et _ _ ll Association
2. MLB Major League B _ _ e _ al _
3. NCAA National Collegiate A _ _ le _ ic Association
4. NFL National F _ o _ _ a _ l League
5. NHL National Hockey L _ a _ _ e

Name/Date ____________________

Sports 2

Match each baseball term to the correct abbreviation.

_____ 1. R _____ 2. ERA

_____ 3. SB _____ 4. BA

_____ 5. CS

a. caught stealing b. runs
c. earned run average
d. batting average e. stolen base

Name/Date ____________________

Sports 3

Circle the basketball word that goes with each abbreviation.

1. H	horse	home	hurt
2. A	away	again	action
3. conf	catch	complete	conference
4. div	defense	dispute	division
5. G	goal	ground	guard

Name/Date ____________________

Sports 4

Fill in the missing football words.

1. W/L wins/____________
2. Y/R ____________ per rush
3. OT over____________
4. QB ____________back
5. RB running____________

Name/Date ____________________

Sports 5

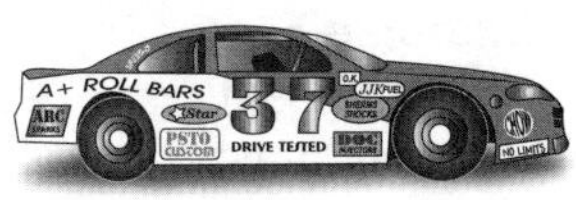

Fill in the missing letters.

1. SF s _ _ ts for
2. SA shots ag _ _ _ s _
3. USFSA United States F _ _ u _ e Ska _ _ ng Association
4. F1 Fo _ _ u _ a 1
5. NASCAR N _ _ ional Association for St _ _ k Car Auto R _ _ ing

Answer Keys

Part I: People and Places

Personal Titles (p. 2)

Exercise 1
1. e 2. d 3. b 4. a 5. c

Exercise 2
1. Esq. 2. Jr. 3. Sr.
4. M.D. 5. D.D.S.

Exercise 3
1. Capt. 2. Gen. 3. Sgt.
4. Col.

Exercise 4
Sentences will vary.

Exercise 5
1. Doctor of Philosophy
2. Registered Nurse
3. Master of Arts
4. Bachelor of Science
5. Bachelor of Arts

Times, Places, and Directions (p. 3)

Exercise 1

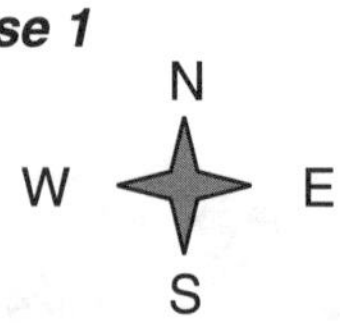

Exercise 2
1. National Park
2. National Monument
3. National
4. National Forest
5. National Wildlife Refuge

Exercise 3
1. fort 2. point 3. river
4. mountains 5. saint

Exercise 4
1. PDT 2. MST 3. CST
4. EDT 5. PST

Exercise 5
1. Northeast 2. Northwest
3. Southeast 4. Southwest
5. Teacher check compass rose.

Continents and Countries (p. 4)

Exercise 1
1. Africa 2. Europe
3. South America 4. Asia
5. Antarctica 6. North America
7. Australia

Exercise 2
1. Fr. 2. Neth. 3. Alg.
4. Belg. 5. Braz.

Exercise 3
1. United States
2. United Kingdom
3. Afghanistan 4. Ethiopia
5. Honduras

Exercise 4
1. e 2. d 3. a 4. b 5. c

Exercise 5
1. Canada 2. Colombia
3. Dominican Republic
4. Switzerland 5. Thailand

Regions and States (p. 5)

Exercise 1
1. South 2. Northeast
3. Midwest 4. West
5. Answers will vary.

Exercise 2
1. DE 2. AZ 3. FL
4. CO 5. GA

Exercise 3
1. Hawaii 2. Idaho 3. Iowa
4. Kansas 5. Louisiana

Exercise 4
1. North Dakota 2. Nevada
3. New Hampshire
4. New Jersey 5. New Mexico

Exercise 5
1. PA 2. TN 3. VT
4. WV 5. OR

States (p. 6)

Exercise 1
1. address 2. sentence
3–4. Answers will vary.

Exercise 2
1. F; CA 2. T 3. F; HI
4. F; KY 5. F; LA

Exercise 3
1. c 2. e 3. b 4. d 5. a

Exercise 4
MI NE OR TN MS IN NV LA ME
MD MA WA SC WI MN DC AZ
ND OH OK IA KS KY PA AR
CA CO MO NH NJ RI VT VA
AL MT WY CT ID IL HI SD DE
FL GA NY NC AK TX UT WV
NM

Exercise 5
1. Arkansas 2. Tennessee
3. Mississippi 4. Maine
5. Wyoming

Highways and Streets (p. 7)

Exercise 1
1. Ave. 2. St. 3. Rd.
4. Blvd. 5. Dr.

Exercise 2
1. Court 2. Circle
3. Expressway 4. Lane
5. Parkway

Exercise 3
1. Place 2. Route
3. Square 4. Terrace 5. Alley

Exercise 4
1. fork 2. bypass 3. camp
4. canyon 5. cove

Exercise 5
1. Anx. 2. Apt. 3. Bsmt.
4. Bch. 5. Bldg.
6. Answers will vary.

People and Places—Mixed Practice (p. 8)

Exercise 1
1. EU 2. Dept. 3. CO
4. Spg. 5. Ave.

Exercise 2
1. Mister 2. Florida
3. Heights 4. Doctor
5. Mountains

Exercise 3
1. Street 2. Gardens
3. Doctor of Philosophy
4. Hawaii 5. Captain

Exercise 4
1. Plains 2. Sergeant
3. Nevada 4. Highway
5. Doctor of Dental Surgery

Exercise 5
1. c 2. d 3. a 4. e 5. b

People and Places—Mixed Practice (p. 9)

Exercise 6
1. Eastern Standard Time
2. North Dakota
3. Mountain Daylight Time
4. Northwest 5. New Jersey

Exercise 7
UT PA WA NH ME MO

Exercise 8
1. Sr. 2. Mrs. 3. Ph.D.
4. Jr. 5. Blvd.

Exercise 9
1. Mr. Edward Collins
2. Stewart Martin, Ph.D.

3. George Williams, Jr.
4. Mrs. Tanya Anderson
5. Dr. Elena Gonzalez

Exercise 10

1. a state name
2. a personal title
3. a street suffix
4. a personal title
5. a state name

People and Places—Mixed Practice (p. 10)

Exercise 11

Sentences will vary.
Miss never uses a period

Exercise 12

Mr. Jason West
223 Hill Ave.
Los Angeles, CA 90040

Exercise 13

1. a dentist 2. a physician
3. a son 4. a wife 5. a man

Exercise 14

1. e 2. d 3. b 4. a 5. c

Exercise 15

Answers will vary.

Part II: Measurement

Hours, Minutes, Days (p. 11)

Exercise 1

1. afternoon
2. morning to afternoon
3. morning to afternoon
4. morning 5. afternoon

Exercise 2

1. Monday 2. Thursday
3. Saturday 4. Wednesday
5. Tuesday 6. Sunday
7. Friday

Exercise 3

1. EDT 2. CST 3. MDT
4. PDT
5. Time zones will vary.

Exercise 4

1. hour 2. minute
3. second 4. Monday
5. Friday

Exercise 5

1–4. Answers will vary.
5. morning

Months (p. 12)

Exercise 1

1. c 2. d 3. e 4. a 5. b

Exercise 2

1. October 2. December
3. August 4. November
5. September

Exercise 3

1. April 2. January
3. August 4. October
5. February

Exercise 4

Spring	Summer	Fall	Winter
Mar.	Jun.	Sept.	Dec.
Apr.	Jul.	Oct.	Jan.
May	Aug.	Nov.	Feb.

Exercise 5

1. True 2. False 3. True
4. True 5. False

Years, Centuries, Millennia (p. 13)

Exercise 1

1. Anno Domini
2. Before Christ
3. Before Common Era
4. Common Era 5. Century

Exercise 2

1. Millenium 2. first century
3. Before the Common Era
4. CE

Exercise 3

Crossed out:
1. Dec. 4 2. Nov. 26
3. Apr. 17 4. Mar. 29

Exercise 4

1. 2010 2. 1980s 3. 1880s
4. 2008 5. 2010's

Exercise 5

1. 100 BCE 2. Nov. 12, 2003
3. 345 BC 4. 1880s
5. Any date before Apr. 2, 2000

Metric Measures (p. 14)

Exercise 1

1. gram 2. kilogram
3. microgram 4. milligram
5. metric ton 6. N

Exercise 2

1. c 2. e 3. d 4. a 5. b

Exercise 3

1. liter 2. centiliter
3. deciliter 4. kiloliter
5. milliliter

Exercise 4

1. millimeter 2. centimeter
3. kilometer 4. meter
5. decimeter

Exercise 5

1. watt 2. kilowatt
3. kilowatt-hour 4. Kelvin
5. Celsius

Standard Measures (p. 15)

Exercise 1

1. square 2. cubic 3. dozen
4. revolutions per minute
5. miles per hour

Exercise 2

1. e 2. c 3. d 4. b
5. a 6. Y

Exercise 3

1. True 2. False 3. True
4. True 5. False

Exercise 4

1. teaspoon 2. tablespoon
3. cup 4. gallon
5. Fahrenheit

Exercise 5

1. nautical miles 2. knot
3. miles per hour 4. quart
5. feet

Standard Measures of Length (p. 16)

Exercise 1

1. yd. 2. ft. 3. mi. 4. in.

Exercise 2

1. square mile 2. square inch
3. square yard 4. square foot/feet
5. T

Exercise 3

1. c 2. b 3. a 4. d

Exercise 4

1. ft. 2. yd. 3. cu. ft.
4. sq. in. 5. sq. ft.

Exercise 5

1. False 2. True 3. False
4. True 5. True

Standard Measures of Volume (p. 17)

Exercise 1

Recipes will vary.

Exercise 2

1. qt. 2. pt. 3. tbsp.
4. gal. 5. c.

Exercise 3

1. c. 2. pt. 3. qt.
4. gal. 5. tbsp.

Exercise 4

1. cup 2. pint
3. quart 4. gallon 5. gal.

Exercise 5
1. perfume 2. detergent
3. milk 4. gasoline
5. cream

Standard Measures Mixed Practice (p. 18)

Exercise 1
1. tons 2. Fahrenheit
3. ounces 4. pounds
5. teaspoons

Exercise 2
1. ounce 2. pound
3. ton 4. dozen

Exercise 3
1. ounce 2. pound
3. ton 4. teaspoon
5. tablespoon

Exercise 4
1. inch 2. ounce 3. pound
4. yard 5. ton

Exercise 5
Answers will vary.

Metric and Standard Mixed Practice (p. 19)

Exercise 1
1. c 2. d 3. b 4. e 5. a

Exercise 2
1. a trip 2. a marathon
3. a football field 4. a hallway
5. a tree

Exercise 3
1. liter 2. quart 3. pint
4. milliliter 5. kiloliter

Exercise 4
1. F 2. C 3. oz. 4. lb.
5. g

Exercise 5
Answers will vary.

Time Mixed Practice (p. 20)

Exercise 1
1. Mon. 2. hr. 3. EST
4. AD 5. BCE

Exercise 2
1. d 2. e 3. a 4. b 5. c

Exercise 3
1. Pacific Daylight Time
2. post meridiem 3. December
4. month
5. Before Common Era

Exercise 4
1. BC 2. a.m. 3. CE
4. p.m. 5. AD

Exercise 5
Answers will vary.

Measurement—Mixed Practice (p. 21)

Exercise 1
1. Pacific Daylight Time
2. pound 3. teaspoon
4. Mountain Standard Time
5. ante meridiem

Exercise 2
1. d 2. e 3. b 4. c 5. a

Exercise 3
1. qt. 2. km 3. yd. 4. gal.
5. pt.

Exercise 4
1. millimeter 2. tablespoon
3. Fahrenheit 4. cup
5. February

Exercise 5
(Any order is acceptable.)
1. Jan. 2. Feb. 3. Mar.
4. Apr. 5. May 6. Jun.
7. Jul. 8. Aug. 9. Sept.
10. Oct. 11. Nov. 12. Dec.

Measurement—Mixed Practice (p. 22)

Exercise 6
1. March 2. Before Christ
3. Feet 4. Tuesday
5. Minute

Exercise 7
1. October 2. kiloliter 3. year
4. gallon 5. cubic

Exercise 8
1. 6:20 a.m. 2. Feb. 16
3. 215 BCE 4. Feb. 20, 2008
5. 10:15 a.m.

Exercise 9
1. December 2. Thursday
3. quart 4. minute
5. February

Exercise 10
Sun. Mon. Tues. Wed.
Thurs. Fri. Sat. (any order)

Measurement—Mixed Practice (p. 23)

Exercise 11
1. ft. 2. lb. 3. gal.
4. sq. ft. 5. cu. ft.

Exercise 12
1. kilometer 2. gallon 3. yard
4. millimeter 5. pint

Exercise 13
1. b 2. d 3. a 4. e 5. c

Exercise 14
1. kilometer 2. gallon
3. mile 4. meter
5. kilogram

Exercise 15
Answers will vary.

Part III: Science and Technology Health and Medicine (p. 24)

Exercise 1
1. c 2. d 3. e 4. a 5. b

Exercise 2
1. a measure of acidity
2. parts per million
3. parts per trillion
4. positive 5. negative

Exercise 3
1. decibel 2. temperature
3. molar 4. blood pressure
5. computed tomography

Exercise 4
1. electrocardiogram
2. female 3. male
4. Doctor of Medicine
5. deoxyribonucleic acid

Exercise 5
1. magnetic resonance imaging
2. weight 3. Fahrenheit
4. hospital
5. health maintenance organization

Weather (p. 25)

Exercise 1
1. cirrostratus 2. cirrus
3. cumulonimbus
4. altocumulus 5. cumulus

Exercise 2
1. b 2. d 3. e 4. a 5. c

Exercise 3
1. inches 2. feet
3. lightning 4. observation
5. National Weather Service

Exercise 4
1. clear 2. drizzle
3. frozen 4. gusts
5. hailstones

Exercise 5
1. fog 2. thunderstorm
3. showers 4. dust storm
5. rain

Elements (p. 26)

Exercise 1
1. hydrogen and oxygen
2. sodium and chlorine

3. carbon and oxygen
4. iron and oxygen
5. sodium, hydrogen, carbon, and oxygen

Exercise 2
1. aluminum 2. americium
3. argon 4. barium
5. calcium

Exercise 3
1. c 2. e 3. b 4. a 5. d

Exercise 4
1. iodine 2. sulfur 3. zinc
4. boron 5. copper

Exercise 5
1. gold 2. silicon
3. uranium 4. silver
5. chlorine

Communications (p. 27)

Exercise 1
1. dots per inch
2. file transfer protocol
3. graphic interchange format
4. global positioning system

Exercise 2
1. c 2. d 3. e 4. a 5. b

Exercise 3
1. IU 2. OCR 3. OS
4. PC 5. URL

Exercise 4
1. digital video disc
2. cycles per second
3. very high frequency
4. electric
5. random access memory

Exercise 5
1. magazine 2. mail
3. network 4. software
5. resistor

Space Science (p. 28)

Exercise 1
1. year 2. Jupiter
3. frequency 4. array
5. white

Exercise 2
1. Andromeda 2. Aquarius
3. Cancer 4. Canis Minor
5. Cassiopeia

Exercise 3
1. e 2. c 3. b 4. a 5. d

Exercise 4
1. satellite 2. universal time
3. center of gravity
4. gravity 5. high frequency

Exercise 5
1. Big 2. Space 3. galaxy
4. Object 5. Units

Science and Technology—Mixed Practice (p. 29)

Exercise 1
1. e 2. c 3. b 4. a 5. d

Exercise 2
1. geology 2. number
3. alternating current
4. atmosphere 5. boiling point

Exercise 3
1. centimeter 2. candlepower
3. central processing unit
4. melting point
5. kinetic energy

Exercise 4
1. hertz
2. revolutions per minute
3. meter 4. volt
5. standard

Exercise 5
1. dots 2. instrument
3. parts 4. direct 5. unit

Science and Technology—Mixed Practice (p. 30)

Exercise 6
1. radio 2. star 3. degree
4. Jet 5. infrared

Exercise 7
1. e 2. c 3. b 4. a 5. d

Exercise 8
1. Andromeda 2. Aquarius
3. Cancer 4. Canis Minor
5. Cassiopeia

Exercise 9
1. ultra high frequency
2. dots per inch
3. internet protocol
4. frequently asked questions
5. global positioning system

Exercise 10
1. inches 2. feet 3. lightning
4. observation
5. National Weather Service

Part IV: Common Acronyms and Initializations (p. 31)

Exercise 1
1. National 2. underwater
3. radiation 4. only
5. normal

Exercise 2
1. radio detection and ranging
2. absent without leave
3. random access memory
4. automated teller machine

Exercise 3
1. delivery 2. personal
3. officer 4. plan

Exercise 4
1. F 2. T 3. F 4. T 5. T

Exercise 5
1. d 2. e 3. a 4. b 5. c

Common Acronyms and Initializations (p. 32)

Exercise 6
1. possible 2. executive
3. accountant 4. information
5. head

Exercise 7
1. central processing unit
2. public address
3. zone improvement plan
4. to be announced
5. sport utility vehicle

Exercise 8
1. ship 2. television
3. important 4. standing
5. quick

Exercise 9
1. T 2. F 3. F 4. T 5. F

Exercise 10
1. known 2. jockey
3. applicable 4. script
5. loving

Part V: Writing Words About Words (p. 33)

Exercise 1
1. e 2. c 3. d 4. a 5. b

Exercise 2
1. suffix 2. pronoun
3. usually 4. spelling
5. pronunciation

Exercise 3
1. participle 2. conjunction
3. object 4. syllable
5. superlative

Exercise 4
1. present participle
2. singular 3. present
4. prefix 5. possessive

Exercise 5
1. plural 2. comparative
3. past tense 4. synonym
5. antonym

Other Dictionary Terms (p. 34)
Exercise 1
1. dialect 2. dictionary
3. diminutive 4. especially
5. except
Exercise 2
1. e 2. d 3. a 4. b 5. c
Exercise 3
1. compound 2. dialect
3. except 4. frequently
5. infinitive
Exercise 4
1. unknown 2. technical
3. standard 4. popularly
5. phrase
Exercise 5
1. infinitive 2. irregular
3. miscellaneous
4. occasionally 5. abbreviation

Latin Terms and Shortened English Words (p. 35)
Exercise 1
1. d 2. a 3. e 4. c 5. b
Exercise 2
1. and others 2. the same
3. rest in peace 4. improvise
5. about
Exercise 3
1. T 2. T 3. F 4. F 5. T
Exercise 4
1. example 2. number
3. figure 4. edition
5. especially
Exercise 5
1. continuing forever
2. so it is shown
3. compare 4. against
5. does not follow

Words About Publications (p. 36)
Exercise 1
1. contents 2. title 3. right
4. pages 5. glossary
Exercise 2
1. page 2. chapter
3. preface 4. translation
5. anonymous
Exercise 3
1. revised 2. Series
3. quotation 4. Publications
5. Quarterly
Exercise 4
1. magazine 2. illustration
3. addenda 4. introduction
5. bibliography
Exercise 5
1. c 2. e 3. a 4. b 5. d

Part VI: Career Track
Business and Finance (p. 37)
Exercise 1
1. T 2. F 3. T 4. F 5. T
Exercise 2
1. Company 2. Corporation
3. Incorporated
4. Limited Partnership
5. Limited
Exercise 3
1. manufacturing 2. railroad
3. railway 4. manager
5. merchandise
Exercise 4
1. e 2. c 3. a 4. d 5. b
Exercise 5
1. account 2. each
3. including 4. paid
5. package

Classified Ads (p. 38)
Exercise 1
1. attorney 2. veterinarian
3. assistant 4. manager
5. principal
Exercise 2
1. c 2. a 3. e 4. d 5. b
Exercise 3
1. accountant 2. practical
3. thousand 4. information
5. references
Exercise 4
1. T 2. F 3. T 4. F 5. F
Exercise 5
1. Saturday and Sunday
2. Monday through Friday
3. paid vacations
4. appointment
5. personnel department

Organizations, Companies, Agencies, and Acts (p. 39)
Exercise 1
1. c 2. e 3. b 4. a 5. d
Exercise 2
1. ABC 2. CBS 3. NBC
4. PBS 5. BBC
Exercise 3
1. Service 2. Federal
3. Postal 4. Disabilities
5. Public
Exercise 4
1. European Union
2. North Atlantic Treaty Organization
3. United Nations
4. Organization of Petroleum-Exporting Countries
Exercise 5
1. Intelligence 2. Investigation
3. Internal 4. Commission
5. Occupational

Education (p. 40)
Exercise 1
1. Reading 2. Science
3. English 4. Association
5. Social
Exercise 2
1. Advanced 2. Learner
3. Language 4. Education
5. Child
Exercise 3
1. B.A. 2. B.E.E. 3. B.F.A.
4. B.N. 5. C.E.
Exercise 4
1. c 2. e 3. b 4. a 5. d
Exercise 5
1. T 2. T 3. T 4. F 5. F

Sports (p. 41)
Exercise 1
1. Basketball 2. Baseball
3. Athletic 4. Football
5. League
Exercise 2
1. b 2. c 3. e 4. d 5. a
Exercise 3
1. home 2. away
3. conference 4. division
5. guard
Exercise 4
1. losses 2. yards
3. time 4. quarter
5. back
Exercise 5
1. shots 2. against
3. Figure Skating
4. Formula 1
5. National Association for Stock Car Auto Racing